Culture DetoX

Cleansing our minds from toxic thinking

Dr Carla Cornelius

Jesus Joy Publishing

First Published and printed in Great Britain in 2010 by
Jesus Joy Publishing a division of Eklegein Ltd

ISBN 978-1-907971-00-6

Jesus Joy Publishing

A division of Eklegein Ltd

www.jesusjoypublishing.co.uk

Dedication

To my Heavenly Father who inspires "the meditations of my heart" and has equipped me with the wisdom and stamina to bring this book to fruition.

To my husband, Michael, you are *"the wind beneath my wings"* without which this book would not have been brought into the public domain.

To my parents, Sir Richard Cheltenham and Dr Hazel Cheltenham, who have fuelled my curiosity about life by their example, and who have always encouraged my writing.

To Mary Blackburn, mentor and friend, you are a rare embodiment of what it means to live unpolluted by this world.

About The Author

Carla Cornelius Ph.D. gained her doctorate in Biblical Counselling from Trinity School of the Bible and Theological Seminary in Newburgh, Indiana. Her dissertation focused on a model for suicide prevention.

At one time her life was immersed in the popular culture but the arrival of her son, Fela, began a search for truth. He was diagnosed with autism at the age of two, precocious puberty at seven and is now 16.

Her previous publication is a devotional, perpetual desk calendar for care-givers called 'Time for Me: encouragement for those caring for others' which was inspired from the ongoing challenges of caring for her special needs son.

Dr. Cornelius resides with her husband, Michael, in Cheshire, England. Their website is to be found at www.jesusjoy.org.uk.

Contents

Introduction

I'm about to enter my third decade of being an adult. With each new decade I have observed and experienced certain trends which for many seem to go unnoticed. If noticed, they seem to go unchallenged except by a small minority who care enough and are unafraid of being labelled as old-fashioned and prudish. I count myself as one of them because I fear that in our attempts to be modern and sophisticated, we are losing our peace of mind and appreciation for the simple, solid values which make life worthwhile and meaningful.

I use the word 'culture' as opposed to 'world' in order to distinguish the constant and insidious perpetuation of societal norms from the current pre-occupation with environmental pollution fuelled by the environmental lobby. Culture refers to "the set of shared attitudes, values, goals, and practices that characterises an institution, organization or group."[1] Indeed, modern society with its shifting values has left us without a clear sense of direction. I will be shining the spotlight on trends, turns and types which have characterised the modern terrain of the final decade of the twentieth century and the first decade of the twenty-first century [1990-2010].

The influences of this era form an overwhelming torrent of bad news and scandals. To prevent ourselves from being swept along on a tide of negative trends, will require a special brand of spiritual discernment to be able to spot and counter-act the lies and propaganda we are being sold particularly through the media. For the majority, it is not a viable alternative to turn our backs on mainstream society, and go and live as recluses on a deserted island. Reassuringly, it is possible to live in the world and yet be unstained by its moral pollutants. Jesus admonished his followers to live as "children of God without blemish in the midst of a crooked and perverse generation."[2] In these days, there is a wave of distortions of truth like never before, making it difficult for the average person to distinguish between right and wrong. The key to avoiding this pitfall is for followers of Jesus everywhere to move beyond religious posturing to an intimate walk with the Lord as in the days of the Acts of the Apostles.

In this period of history, spiritual toxins come from many sources and directions. For example, the proliferation of technology such as mobile phones and satellite television makes it difficult just to concentrate on one thought for a significant period of time. Our minds are constantly exposed to the threat of distraction. No military invasion has so much at stake. When the Berlin wall came down in 1989, it may have seemed that the West's enemy of communism had fallen, but since that time there have been even more powerful spiritual enemies which have emerged within the nations of the West. These forces which often work through people, use the very culture to which we are accustomed and which makes us feel safe, to undermine our moral standards. Western culture faces more danger from within, through the steady erosion of the core values upon which it has been built, than from nuclear detonation by a foreign power. For example, newspapers have become so celebrity-focused that it's easy to miss the point of what's really going on and what truly matters. Do you not often wonder why the world is set up like this? To illustrate the extent of our mass delusions, Princess Diana's sudden, tragic death in 1997 exposed, amongst other things, the extent to which the public en masse had come to regard her as an intimate even though the vast majority had never met her in person. For most, their exposure to her had been courtesy of television and the print media.

The ancient Greeks had four words for love – *eros, philia, storge, and agape*. Notably, they did not recognise the adulation of a famous person as a form of love. Today, we often like to ooze our regard for a certain celebrity with the words "I love...." Such professions of undying adulation were rife after the recent death of Michael Jackson. It is more probable that his fans were addicted to the temporary buzz his music imparted but could not disengage the flawed and intriguing man from his flawless musical and performing legacy. The question arises – why do we get more excited by the public dramas of life such as the election of Barack Obama as American president, the X-factor finals, or World Cup football, than we do by the circumstances and events in our own private lives? We seem to have become alienated from our own realities.

I use the word 'disciple of Christ', 'follower of Jesus' or any variation thereof as opposed to 'Christian' - a term which was first used in a derogatory fashion by those who opposed Christianity.[3] The term seems to have come full circle, and has now become associated with the fundamentalist religious right, nominal faith or religious hypocrisy. Neither accurately reflects the message of Christ, and what he represented. It is hoped that this book will help you to see Christ through fresh, less stereotypical lenses. It is also hoped that after reading this book, you will be less inclined to let the failings of those who peddle the name, turn you off the greatness of Christ himself and the relevance of his message for all people and all times.

Chapter 1

Greed & Materialism

The main criterion for measuring success in modern times seems to be how much money you make. This is evidenced by the proliferation of 'Rich Lists' such as the 'Sunday Times Rich List', the 'Forbes Rich List' and the 'Ten highest paid hedge fund managers of 2008'. Those reading these lists allow themselves to be sucked in by the veneer of power and prestige - an opulent lifestyle where nothing is beyond their buying power. It is to this glossy ideal that most aspire.

We tend to stereotype wealth as the gateway to peace and satisfaction. We have all been guilty of settling for inaccurate stereotypes. **We have become so enamoured of the illusion that wealth brings happiness, that we don't challenge this stereotype despite the overwhelming evidence to the contrary**. Stereotyping, or what's commonly known as generalising, is the symptom of a closed mind and severely restricts our opportunities for spiritual growth and maturity. How can we presume to know others purely on the basis of their appearance , status or income - all external factors that can never accurately reflect what someone is genuinely like or how they feel? We should never presume for example that those who make substantially less money than we do, have nothing worthwhile to offer us. The New Testament book of James delivers a strong condemnation of such presumption - "For if a person with gold rings and in fine clothes comes into your assembly , and if a person in dirty clothes also comes in, and if you take notice of the one wearing the fine clothes and say 'Have a seat here, please' , while to the one who is poor you say, 'Stand there', or, 'Sit at my feet' , have you not made distinctions ...and become judges with evil thoughts?"[4] By making rash judgements based on superficial evidence, we have made ourselves susceptible to being duped or misled. A classic example would be for a woman to assume that a good-looking man comes from a well-educated background simply because he dresses in a suit and tie and drives a Jaguar. The truth is that how we perceive others says more about us than about them.

Where the sensitive issue of money is concerned, rich people rarely socialise with the poor, the stereotype being that the rich person will patronise the poor person and the poor person will exploit the rich one. This is a shame because no-one's worth should be evaluated in terms of what they own, how much money they earn or their credit rating.

The greatest distraction to serving God is money and the pursuit of wealth. Jesus emphatically stated that "you cannot serve God and wealth."[5] The ancient word used for wealth was 'mammon' which is defined as "the personification of riches and greed in the form of a false god" [Concise English Dictionary, New ed.s.v. "mammon"]. Materialism is the constant quest for more things in the hope that they will make us happy. The rich young man who wanted to follow Jesus was told to first go and sell all he had and give it to the poor. Sadly he chose not to follow Jesus because he considered it too high a sacrifice to make. Jesus does not require all his followers to take a vow of poverty but he does challenge us to remove all false gods from our hearts in order to follow him. As *The Beatles* astutely sang in one of their lyrics "I don't care too much for money 'cause money can't buy me love." Indeed, it is love not money which makes the world go around. **Greed and lust take, but true love gives**. The world is not lacking in money or resources to solve its problems but in the motivating factor of love which sees other peoples' needs as equally if not more important than one's own.

What's In A Name?

Today there is an élite group of people worldwide who have achieved such a degree of renown that they are instantly recognised by one name whether it be a first name such as Oprah, Tiger or Madonna; a double barrel abbreviation such as J-Lo, Lilo; and (as with certain celebrity couples) a homogenisation of both names such as Brangelina or Tomkat; or a title such as 'The King of Pop', 'the Queen of Soul' or 'Old Blue

Eyes'.

Many like to attribute wealth and status to divine blessing. But the truth is that worldly success may be achieved through ungodly means. It's easy to adopt the cultural tendency to admire the success of those in the spotlight and give God the glory for the lucrative use of their talents. But we must not lose sight of the fact that talents may be used for good or evil and do not always glorify God. Let us not forget that when the devil tempted Jesus in the wilderness, he offered him "all the kingdoms of the world and their glory"[6] on the condition that he fall down and worship him. There are many people who prosper materially in this world who neither believe in nor worship God. It is dangerous to conclude that just because those in the public eye have acknowledged Jesus Christ in some way and at some time in their career, and they have amassed worldly prestige and wealth, or that they attend church every Sunday that God has favoured them because of their devotion to Him. Indeed, we are told that God blesses all men – the godly and the ungodly alike.[7] You may wonder - how then can one distinguish God's genuine blessings from counterfeit blessings. Proverbs tells us that "the blessing of the Lord makes rich, and he adds no sorrow with it."[8] **The Hebrew understanding of prosperity was much more balanced that the western, capitalist view. It included such factors as physical health, harmonious family relationships and a good standing in the community.** What is the point of amassing loads of money if your health has suffered, your family has been ravaged by divorce and estrangement, you have few or no real friends and a bad reputation. Nowadays there are so many dubious ways to make money. There must be boundaries on our sense of enterprise if we want to maintain a clear conscience and the respect of our fellow-men. Sadly many who are rich and famous become addicted to the adulation of the majority who kowtow to them simply because they have status and power.

Let us for a moment turn the spotlight on the condition of our own hearts. Which of the acts listed below would you be willing to do for money?

- Sell one of your organs.
- Remove your clothes for perfect strangers to gawk.
- Dance immodestly and suggestively in front of perfect strangers.
- Have foreign substances injected into your body to make you look more 'sexy' so you could attract more work in the glamour industry.
- Sell mortgages to people who couldn't afford them.
- Sell legal or illegal drugs which harm others.
- Sleep with a perfect stranger.
- Terminate the life of a foetus who would

inconvenience your career.

The irony is that in poorer nations of the world, there are those who engage in these activities through sheer desperation to make ends meet, while in the richer nations, many regard it as a lifestyle choice. Some of these options may be less revolting than others, or perhaps none seem revolting at all. Would you sell your soul to the devil in exchange for worldly advancement, regardless of how costly the price? This cost may come in terms of:

- Lowered self-esteem as occurs with people who sleep their way to the top.
- Broken family relationships where a workaholic works day and night to make a fortune.
- A health crisis due to neglect of the body's need for sleep, a balanced diet and relaxation.
- Anxiety and loss of peace of mind because you have a gambling or shopping addiction, and your debts are spiralling out of control.

Often those who have attained such success may not even be aware that they have endangered their souls, such is the strength of the pull towards materialism. This is why Christ's followers are warned "Do not love this world nor the things it offers you, for when you love the world, you do not have the love of the Father in you. For the world only offers a craving for physical pleasure, a craving for everything we see, and pride in our achievements and possessions."[9] Indeed, this question has resounded through the generations of humanity since the garden of Eden – "what does it profit a man if he gain the whole world but loses his soul?" Followers of Jesus are encouraged to be content with food and clothing.[10] So many today who claim to follow Jesus would consider food and clothing to be inadequate to meet their needs. They have added on other criteria for contentment such as:

- Good job
- Quality education
- Home ownership
- An affluent neighbourhood
- The latest model of your preferred car
- Substantial savings and investments
- One or two foreign holidays per year
- Happy marriage or coupledom
- Healthy, well-behaved children.

We have virtually guaranteed a constant state of delayed satisfaction as we embark on the ceaseless treadmill of wanting more.

What Are The Fruit?

The ultimate test of an authentic disciple of

Christ is the character which emerges in the most challenging of circumstances when it's most tempting to compromise one's code of ethics for material gain. There are many who have professed faith in Jesus Christ but have not demonstrated this faith with a change in behaviour or lifestyle. They began the faith journey with high hopes and lofty intentions but allowed my cares, distractions and deceptive priorities to take the place of Jesus along the way

The world of celebrity is fraught with obstructions to Christ-like maturity, and both celebrities and their adoring fans can become entangled in this web of false hype and misguided loyalties. The 'yes-men' employed in the entourages of the famous are unlikely to challenge them when they may be tempted to indulge in risky or deleterious activities. They are in a position to afford almost whatever their hearts fancy, and so too they can buy the silence of those who might otherwise object to their rowdy or self-indulgent behaviours. God is often sidelined in favour of money which becomes the chief motivator and justifier for all their actions. Many famous performers who profess faith in Christ have acquired much adoration from their fans and recognition and applause from their peers in the music industry. But a closer examination of some of the lyrics of their songs, reveal messages which do not strengthen Christ-centred morals but openly defy them. Is there a different standard of behaviour for those who claim unfettered artistic license and wild alter egos than there is for the regular Christ follower? Those who profess faith in Christ must ensure that all areas of their lives truthfully portray the lifestyle which Christ promoted even if it means the sacrifice of their wealth or celebrity.

Who Gets The Glory?

It is not considered 'cool' to give glory to Jesus in the performing industry whose values focus on mass exposure and approval in order to ensure maximum profits. The name Jesus is more frequently used as a swear word, regrettably, than out of sacred reverence for God Almighty. Christ followers are warned that the name of Jesus will bring offence, and that those who bear the name will be singled out for persecution and ridicule by the masses. Songs which speak of sexual promiscuity, gender-bending and bashing and unabashed lust can never qualify as promoting Christ-centred values and morals. Yet they are many who have interpreted God's grace so widely that it excuses their most liberal views and actions.

Starting Well, Ending Well

The writer of Ecclesiastes makes it clear that "better is the end of a thing than its beginning."[11] Indeed, it is not how one begins but how one ends that really matters. There are many like Whitney Houston[12] and Natalie Cole[13] who have self-confessedly paid a terrible price by selling their souls to the false values of the music industry. They began in church but soon found themselves caught up in a world of celebrity and negative associations where it was difficult to distinguish between right and wrong. They have lived to share wonderful testimonies of how God was able to deliver them from drug addiction, and they seem to be keen to use their singing talents to glorify Him rather than themselves. We must pray for them and for all those in the public eye who have professed faith in Christ but whose lifestyles leave huge question marks about the genuineness of their faith. No-one, celebrity or otherwise, is above the wiles of the devil to replace God with idols of wealth, fame, and prestige. Perhaps when Christ followers stop idolising these celebrities and the false values they embrace, and instead pray for them, we will see fewer tragedies of such lives derailed or needlessly cut short.

Money, Money, Money

Money is neither good nor bad, but a means to an end. Of itself, money is meaningless - it is we who attach personal meaning to it. The means by which we get it, and the ends for which we use it may, nevertheless, be positive or negative. Mugging old-aged pensioners, robbing banks and destroying the environment would undoubtedly be considered 'foul' means, whereas giving money to charity, paying our bills and taxes, and saving for a rainy day, would generally be considered 'fair'. Poverty is viewed by many as a 'crime' because not having money is associated with shame. As a result, so many crimes are committed to obtain money. On the other hand, having money in abundance, is widely viewed as an injustice in a world so rife with poverty. The irony is that we cannot eradicate poverty unless we create wealth, but not from stealing which can itself lead to want, but through honest, hard, self-sustaining work where everybody wins.

We have fallen 'hook, line and sinker' for the lie that money can buy anything despite the old cliché that 'money can't buy me love'. **Money gives the illusion of control. If you're sick, you can buy medicine, if you're sad, you can buy entertainment, if you are lonely you can buy friends.** You can live where you like, eat and wear what you like. Journalist Maggie Morgan highlights the nineties trend of couples to put off or forego having children to maintain their lifestyles. This does not just relate to the upper middle class but includes those who fear for their economic security and desire early retirement. Though logical, it remains a short-sighted plan. When they are older, all the money in the world will not buy them the love and care only children are in a position to provide. There is never any guarantee that your children will be alive, live close enough to you, or want to care for an ageing parent, but most raised with a modicum of decency and love, will want to be there to help support their parents to some degree through these difficult years. Furthermore, the concept of retiring early so as to fritter away one's life in an endless round of leisure activities, contradicts the basic need of humans to feel good about themselves by engaging in purposeful, worthwhile activities –whether paid or voluntary.

The biblical model for family life is one of strong, extended families where there is always someone to care for the needs of the more vulnerable members of the clan. Jemima Khan observed from her sojourn in Pakistan the strong extended families which ensure the nurturing of secure and stable children. She poses the question of which culture is more barbaric – one where fractured families and individualism are the order of the day, or ones where families live together in mutual respect and harmony, sharing family values and responsibilities?

The divide between rich and poor grows ever wider, fulfilling Jesus' prophecy that the poor would always be around and in need of charity.[14] The entertainment industry, one of the largest wealth-producing industries, displays its wealth with increasing measures of flamboyance. Due largely to the television, internet and print media, we are exposed more than ever to these excesses. This serves to whet the appetite of ordinary people who are feverishly trying to attain exceptional levels of wealth, to 'keep up with the Joneses' and who are prepared to take on crippling debt to give the appearance of wealth. MTV has launched a variation on its popular show *Cribs* which saw the camera expose the splendid excesses of celebrity homes, by now focusing on *Teen Cribs* – homes which have been remodelled and renovated to cater to rich kids. This is meant to target MTV youth globally who will no doubt develop an unrealistic appetite for luxury and a massive sense of discontentment from an early age**. Many bemused and frustrated parents will never be able to satisfy the wish-lists of their increasingly materialistic offspring.**

How Much Is Enough?

Too much of anything will engender monotony and discontent. Fans of Tiger Woods struggled to come to terms with the shocking adulterous revelations of this mere mortal who had been deified as a god for his golfing prowess.[15] The difficulty arose from reconciling the damning evidence of serial adultery with the pristine image of family man that he had projected. He is a sporting billionaire, not just a golfer but a brand used to promote all kinds of products. He represented the epitome of achievement, having acquired an illustrious career with gorgeous wife and children in toe. The fact that he was willing to risk all these on sexual dalliances, suggest that deep down inside, he was discontented and unfulfilled. Money and prestige failed to fill the inner longings for validation. In the words of Rabbi Shmuley "success and a feeling of specialness, were always outside him. He had to devour first championships, and later women, to prove himself worthy."[16]

The need for balance in the human life cannot be over-emphasised. Any exceptional achievement in one area of life usually comes at the sacrifice of other areas. Knowing this, it is no wonder that God encourages us to be self-controlled. Self-control is the last-mentioned fruit of the Spirit, but by no means the least important. **Most things in life are good in moderation, but if taken to extreme, become harmful and unhealthy.** With God, it's different. We can never get enough of Him.

At this moment in history websites exist on the internet teaching people how to marry rich. The holy institution of marriage is being used as a bargaining chip for greedy folk to satisfy their material lusts. Such people are obsessed with the fantasy or image of wealth. One such website promotes the female caricature that you must conform to the physical proportions and appearance of a Barbie doll to attract the attentions of a wealthy man. It falsely assumes that rich men are only interested in eye candy or style over substance. The more telling criterion of being able to love and be loyal "for richer or poorer, 'til death do us part" does not seem to factor in their list.

For the majority, wealth has proven to be an

elusive fantasy they have created which overlooks the challenges of wealth in reality. It's not all it's cracked up to be. Those with much money have a greater responsibility to steward it wisely and effectively. Furthermore, Jesus warned that "from everyone to whom much has been given, much will be required; and from one to whom much has been entrusted, even more will be demanded."[17] Indeed, we come into this world and leave it without any material assets. And so, it makes sense to view everything we gain as simply on loan. As Job lamented "I was naked when I was born, and I will be naked when I die."[18]

Chapter 2

The Cult Of Celebrity

My Story

I grew up with many media idols. As a child whenever I felt nervous or inadequate, I would seek relief and escapism through television. Often the actors or TV personalities I watched week in and week out, possessed qualities I longed to possess; but instead of trying to develop these qualities in myself, I became a stagnant and passive voyeur (the easy option). I thereby robbed myself of the satisfaction of striving for and achieving goals in my own life.

Growing up in the Caribbean, I was exposed to a lot of American television. At one point I had developed such an addiction to the CBS series *Knots Landing* (specifically Paige Matheson, played by Nicolette Sheridan) that if I missed one episode, my whole day was ruined. Paige was young, beautiful and ruthlessly pursuing her own ambition. At the time I felt powerless to pursue mine. I used to religiously watch *Cagney and Lacey*, another American television series, making sure to tape the episodes so that I could play them back and not miss any significant moments. I was mesmerised by Cagney's passion for her work and her fierce independence. By focusing fanatically on these qualities, I could possess them vicariously for a short while, before having to face the sober reality of my own deficiencies. I didn't know it at the time but I was watering the seeds of inadequacy and inferiority which would yield a harvest in later years. Anytime life would get too tough or taxing, I could take refuge in my imagination. This habit became my idol because I replaced the Lord who alone is worthy to be a "refuge."[19] **The danger is that if we do not wrestle with and overcome our idols, they have the potential of pre-occupying our thoughts and lives for a life-time.** If we are captive to images, the fact that these images can be preserved for countless generations in multi-media format, means that they are not going to just go away, but will rear their ugly heads in the magazines and newspapers we read, the billboards we see when we're driving and the advertisements on TV and the internet. They have become part and parcel of our cultural wall-paper so we must determine to overcome them no matter how long it takes.

By indulging these idols, I was putting my dreams on hold for many years while I fixated on these fictional characters, wondering whether I would ever achieve their confidence, social ease and accomplishments. The voices in my head I had tuned into in childhood, would intermittently plague me for many years to come. Such voices can have a demonic hold over you. They may whisper – 'you are fat, ugly, insignificant, incompetent.' So few of us have a sufficiency of opposing statements to counteract these messages.

It's God's Word which provides the truth of just how precious and capable we are. As impressionable children we may imbibe false messages, through lack of verbal affirmation or positive body language from the adults upon whom we depend, and this may in turn shape the way we see ourselves. So few of us feel we have strong enough friendships or social support systems through which to air these falsehoods and have them corrected. When a young girl can feel free to say "I feel fat" or "I feel ugly" to her sister, mother or friend, how they respond can make a huge difference to her self-image. When we dismiss peoples' feelings as silly or insignificant, eventually they will feel so rejected and devalued that they stop sharing them. **The broken self-image is eventually replaced with a false image of 'perfection' - the 'stars' in the world who seem to attract all the praise and affirmation and who seem to exude confidence from every pore.**

Children are being increasingly sold these falsified images of perfection through advertising. A paediatric study revealed that children are exposed to 40 000 TV adverts in a year[20]. The rate at which these images are being sown into our children's hearts is cause for alarm. Silently and seductively they are being set up for a lifetime of not feeling good enough, and looking to the external world to feed their self-esteem whether it be acquisition of material possessions, obsession with their appearance or the hunger for power and fame. For so many this sense of power will not be attained by glowing achievement, but through bullying, gang violence, addiction to drugs and alcohol or eating disorders.

We should never regard another human being as more significant than ourselves, least of all a fictional character, because in God's eyes we're all of equal value. Why strive to be like a flawed human-being when you can follow Jesus - the only 'God-man' who led a perfect life[21] and who created you as you are for a reason? Indeed, "all things were made through him, and without him nothing was made that was made."[22]

All these TV idols are ultimately flawed. In the eighties I remember being captivated by the supermodel, Cindy Crawford, ecstatic when she married the actor, Richard Gere, and crushed when their marriage broke up. My interests were swiftly diverted elsewhere because when one human disappoints us, knowingly or unknowingly, our attention is refocused on someone else, only to be disappointed again. And so the cycle continues until we come to our senses. But sadly, some never do. Indeed, the basic human need to trust someone or something is inescapable. God made us to rely on Him to fill those massive shoes, and none other.

For the better part of my life, I've been an ardent collector of newspaper clippings on the rich and famous. I rationalised to myself that somehow being privy to their lives would inspire me to make a success of my own life. I know now that at a deeper level, I wanted to be them, to live those lives so glamorously portrayed. Being myself seemed too drab and unfulfilling so I sought refuge in escapism. I've now learned that it's equally unfulfilling to escape into something that's all hype and smokescreens. Furthermore, **we can never truly succeed at being someone else, only ourselves**. On the surface the celebrity lifestyle looks cool and worthy of emulation, but often it's an empty shell with no substance. Celebrity can be a force for good or evil but of itself it means nothing except the fact that more people know your name. Essentially, we are all the same whether millions know our name or just a few. We often struggle to find out who we are, why we're here, where we belong, and what to do with our most valuable and expendable commodity - time.

Idolatry In Disguise

An idol is not limited to a golden image or a religious icon, it is in essence "anything we put before God in our lives. It is what we love, like, trust, desire, or give our attention to more than the Lord. An idol is what you draw your strength from or give your strength to."[23] We expect it to give us benefits only God can confer such as peace of mind, contentment and meaning. In 2001, I briefly heard on the radio the results of a survey on fame stating that Britney Spears was considered to be more famous than

Jesus Christ. This struck me as being propaganda more than truth since Jesus Christ has influenced men down through the ages while this pop star had not even attained the age of majority. Similarly, in the wake of Barrack Obama's historic election as President of USA in 2009, a Harris poll found him to be a more popular hero than Jesus Christ.[24] These examples only serve to illustrate how dominant the celebrity culture is today. Nowadays being a celebrity is tantamount to being deified as a god. The light of truth put this trend in perspective - "when you did not know God, you served those which by nature are not gods"[25]. The truth is that no human being can be compared to God's fame which preceded mankind's existence. Indeed, He is known by the angels, the planets and all of His creation from eternity past into eternity future.[26]

There are an ever-growing number of magazines dedicated to chronicling every move that celebrities make such as **Hello** and **OK**! It has gotten to the point where other types of publications seek to hitch a ride on the celebrity bandwagon by dedicating a section, no matter how small, to a celebrity in order to promote a cause or make a point. The likelihood is their sales will increase even though they have fed the flames of idolatry which is sweeping through the globe unchecked and blinding human hearts to the real God. The argument by the press and paparazzi that celebrities are fair game for media attention and invasion, whether they are on or off duty, is due primarily to the overwhelming public demand for the smallest detail about their lives. No wonder the reporters satisfy this demand in often demeaning and detestable ways, and sometimes propagate false stories to whet the public appetite for celebrity scandal.

If you trace your idols over your lifetime, you realise that they are always changing. Perhaps they age and become less attractive, or die; or the boy band splits up leaving you disillusioned; or the celebrity couple you think had it all together, split up, thereby shattering the illusion of everlasting domestic bliss. In most cases, they become less news-worthy or have stepped out of the limelight. The media abhors a vacuum so they are immediately replaced by another celebrity who is younger, with star quality and who shows creative, sporting or musical promise. Everyone likes to think they've backed a winner, including the press. It doesn't matter whether they are perennially glamorous like Joan Collins or a die-hard rock band such as *The Rolling Stones*, they will begin to fade in the public imagination as the media turn their attentions elsewhere.

There is also the issue of human fickleness. When we are overwhelmed with information and photos of a 'star', there comes a point when we become sick of it like too much honey. We have a natural tendency to crave variety. Those idols we once adored no longer look so appealing because we have become too familiar with their image. All our senses operate that way. We eat too much cheese cake for too long, listen to a song or CD too many times, and eventually we will not be able to stand it anymore. Indeed, familiarity does breed contempt. At the root of our celebrity obsessions is the fact that we view them as neatly packaged 'images' or brands separate from their core humanity. We view them through rose-tinted glasses and don't like to think that they have the same experiences we do such as bad hair days, boredom, heartache and sickness; and even if they do, they rebound from them with magical speed. By so doing, we have essentially de-humanised them. Our media-fuelled perceptions trap us into sustaining illusions about others which shield us from the truth. Discovering the truth would probably shatter our illusions – a blessing in disguise.

The Pursuit Of Fame

If you ask many youngsters today what they want to be when they grow up, they will say 'famous', as if fame is a justifiable goal in itself. A survey found that the top three aspirations of 5-11 year olds in Britain were "sports star, pop star and actor." **Fame can never be a worthy goal in itself but is the product of doing something well.** By contrast, there is such a thing as 'infamy' which means celebrity for doing something evil such as the dictator, Adolf Hitler who masterminded the genocide of the Jews during the

Second World War or Harold Shipman, the serial killer General Practitioner in England who killed several of his patients. But this term has become almost obsolete because now all that counts is celebrity, whether it's positive or negative. There have been recent incidences of mass murder accompanied or followed by the suicide of the perpetrator as with terrorist attacks and gun rampages. It is likely that these crimes are motivated by more than just hatred or revenge, but also the sure knowledge by the perpetrators that their crimes will make them famous. Fame has become the sought-after drug to be attained in life or death. The same goes for the macabre incidences where people have filmed their suicides for broadcast on the internet. Many have become deluded enough to believe they will live on in cyber history , have their names written in the cyber hall of fame or have glowing tributes posted on their facebook walls for the 'world' to read.

This also accounts for the current trend in programmes such as **X Factor**, **Britain's Got Talent** and **Big Brother**. Ordinary people, dissatisfied with the mundaneness of their own existences, are trying their best to secure fifteen minutes of fame as if this will satisfy the deep longings of their souls forever. Why this need for publicity and excessive attention? Have the older generations not done a good enough job of making the younger generations aware of their inherent worth? Unfortunately, so many of us were stripped of our innate sense of self-worth by thoughtless or uncaring adults during our impressionable childhoods. So we spend the rest of our lives trying to recover from this broken self-image, the result being a frenetic search for external validation.

It is no surprise that many celebrities sought the limelight because of an unhealthy need (stemming from childhood dysfunctions) to be loved. In Madonna's critically-acclaimed album 'Ray of light', she sings about fame as her "substitute for love."[27] Having lived so many years with fame and in the pursuit of it, she finally concluded that it could not fulfil her longing for love. Marilyn Monroe, was quoted as saying "I want to be a big star more than anything." She had been abandoned by her father and spent most of her childhood in foster homes due to her mother's mental illness.[28] Marvin Gaye was a study in contradictions. A preacher's son, his lyrics were infused with spirituality, but their sexual overtones also reflected his pre-occupation with sex. Although he craved the adoration of female fans, he dreaded performing and considered it belittling. He was also angst-ridden about his commercial success which never seemed to satisfy him, but which he relied upon to try to gain his father's approval.[29]

The character portrayed by Nicole Kidman in the movie *To Die For*, made the memorable statement–"You're a nobody unless you're on TV."[30] As silly as it sounds, it rings surprisingly true in this Age of craving for celebrity. The press coverage given to celebrities, many of whom are only famous for being famous without any substantial achievement or mark of excellence, only serves to feed this public misconception. Kidman's character in the film may seem so twisted and far removed from reality that we can dismiss her as a fictional caricature. Yet this kind of thinking is becoming prevalent in today's popular culture. It accounts for the proliferation of talk shows such as the *Jeremy Kyle* or *Jerry Springer* shows where ordinary folk seek out the public domain of television to air their dirty linen.

The True Meaning Of Success

Those who succeed in any worthwhile field or endeavor have paid their dues with diligence and determination for which they deserve our respect and admiration. Nevertheless, we must resist any inclination towards idolatry, envy or even resentment because success always comes at a price - sacrifice, failure and frustration. Indeed, for many, the price may have simply been too high. These wise words of Jesus resound through the ages - "What does it profit a man to gain the whole world and lose his soul?" [31] Each individual is a link in a human chain; there are those who have preceded us and those who will follow us in the progression of time. Indeed, anyone who inspires or facilitates our ambitions such as a mentor, deserves our humble respect and gratitude.

Nevertheless, we must guard against our gratitude becoming idolatry or hero worship. The Bible warns emphatically "...keep yourselves from idols."[32] Whereas a mentor inspires growth by encouraging us to become the best we can be, idol-worship encourages obsession which means that we neglect our own lives and personal development. This is harmful insomuch as our efforts at self-improvement are put on hold as we fixate on an external illusion of perfection. By contrast, the worship of God is never passive. It shines a spotlight on the dark places of our hearts, and as we look into the mirror[33] of God's Word, we are compelled to seek His forgiveness and grace to become transformed. **Acknowledging the reality of our spiritual condition is when the truly great God moments can occur.**

The Good Book states that belief is insufficient since "even the devils believe."[34] Our belief in God must be backed up by action - "faith without works is dead."[35] Our perceptions of our idols are often skewed and our adoration all-encompassing, and so we risk losing our sense of identity and reality. With a mentor we become a better version of ourselves and not merely a fanatic. So often people are labelled successes by others yet when many celebrities are interviewed, we see them for what they are – riddled with discontent, insecurity or arrogance. Very rarely do they ooze happiness. It's no wonder - would you be happy having to look over your shoulder all the time in case a camera got shoved in your face, to have to sign autographs for perfect strangers who have no reservation about disturbing you in the middle of a private moment. Add to this picture the following – having to become a prisoner in your own home because of the possibility of being accosted by fawning fans or the paparazzi; or worse yet, having to employ an entourage of bodyguards or personal assistants to accompany your every move, with the lingering suspicion they might sell their story to the press once their service is no longer required. The decision is difficult – continue this bizarre lifestyle of public adulation or become a 'nobody' again. Yet, there are those who have decided to reject these 'accoutrements' of celebrity, and who still go to the local supermarket, drive their own cars, or dare to be photographed in normal attire without makeup. Being famous brings in coveted work and money, being a 'nobody' means giving up a lifestyle which boosts your ego and keeps you in a lifestyle of luxury you could only have dreamed of as a child and which your peers envy. So many choose to "gain the whole world, but lose [their] soul."[36] Secretly, they may feel like frauds. They are perfectly aware of more talented, beautiful people around, and know in their hearts that their success is attributable to so many factors and co-incidences beyond their control. Those who come to this awareness, become painstakingly aware that they are not as fabulous or perfect as people make them out to be.

This is probably why so many celebrities are

acting out in bizarre and uncouth ways. The reckless behaviour of the likes of Britney Spears, Paris Hilton and Amy Winehouse may be a defiant attempt to 'keep it real'. Tired of being told how wonderful they are, they probably chafe at the responsibility of having to live up to the public's idealised expectations of them. **No human being was created for adulation**. It will either go to your head and give you an inflated ego or it will magnify your insecurities. Most celebrities are reluctant ones, uncomfortable with the demands of the media glare. The media ought to leave them alone. They are not true public servants like our elected officials. Most give autographs grudgingly, and surround themselves with bodyguard 'thugs' to distance themselves from their fans. They were in it for the money or for ego-massaging but not because they really love people and want to help them. Jesus was the antithesis of this, although a celebrity in his own right. Indeed, Jesus always gave glory to God the Father. More celebrities ought to nip 'hero worship' in the bud with humility and modesty, as opposed to encouraging it through boasting and flamboyant lifestyles. The purpose of wealth is always to spread it not hoard it or indulge in hedonistic excesses which destroy and cut short the lives of those who are deceived by them.

Good Reputation

What will you be celebrated for? John Ruskin, the

English writer (1819-1900), wrote that **"the weakest among us has a gift, however seemingly trivial, which is peculiar to him, and which worthily used, will be a gift to his race forever."** I can think of no better motivation – not just to be known by as many as possible, but to be known(by your circle of family, friends and associates) and celebrated for something worthwhile that will endure. Let's begin to look at reality from God's eyes, not through the media lens which so often distorts the truth. Disciples of Christ, regardless of nationality, ethnicity, gender and age are the real "stars"[37] on earth. There is no star on Hollywood Boulevard that can outshine them.

Lusting After Lifestyle

Very often, it's the trappings of celebrity which seduce us. The images of being chauffeured in limousines, not having to stand in queues, first class travel and exotic holidays, feed our lust for easier, more luxurious lifestyles. Very few of us consider the hard work and drive involved in attaining or maintaining such a lifestyle. We also tend to forget the true value of work – not amassing wealth for our own self-indulgence but to be of service to others. Yet it is service not image that will always be appreciated because human need is an inexhaustible well. **Most people who are doing good and being good examples will not capture the attention of the media for a long time, if at all.** In fact the profits of much of the media rely on the public appetite for the scandalous and salacious. This usually involves perversions of sex, drugs and money. We are so bombarded with images in this culture that our imaginations have gone haywire. We are less captivated by godly examples of self-sacrifice and self-discipline because they show up our shortcomings and challenge our complacency.

World events of huge magnitude are pushed off the front pages of the tabloid press for the more trivial coverage of celebrity foibles and antics and 'do's and don'ts'. **We live in an age where people seem to be more interested in what Victoria Beckham is wearing than the starving millions in developing nations. We are more pre-occupied with Jennifer Aniston's hair than the state of our nation with its moral decay and social inequities.** Although we can blame the paparazzi, editors and publishers alike for taking the photos and running these stories, we have only ourselves to fault for fuelling the demand by buying the newspapers and magazines and tuning into the programmes. It raises the question of how we the buying public, whether adoring fans or curious voyeurs, view ourselves since we are clearly so eager to live vicariously through celebrities and put them on pedestals like virtual gods. It may be that we are suffering from a surfeit of bad news – the starving millions, crimes of violence and economic recession – such that we crave escape. **The bad news leaves us feeling powerless because there is too much**

of it. The showbiz news gives us a temporary relief as we momentarily forget the state of the world. We have become escapist junkies. We are constantly tempted to escape into a world of make-believe from which there often seems no escape. For example, the 1997 VH1 fashion awards was a colourful blend of fashionistas, movie A-listers and pop melody-makers. Apart from the prizes, viewers could have been forgiven for forgetting which industry was being fêted. Indeed, these industries – fashion, film and music - have become almost indivisible in modern times. Nowhere is this more evident than the Oscars and Grammies where just as much of a hullaballoo is made about which designers they are wearing, as the work of art for which they are being recognised. Ecclesiastes tells us that "a threefold cord is not quickly broken"[38] – a principles which applies in every sector of life.

Seduced By The Glitz And Glamour

Fashion is everywhere. At any given day, at any given moment, in any given town, you can catch a glimpse of a fashionista. They are ordinary men and women from all walks of life, spanning all income brackets and ages. What is it about these folk that make them fashionable? They are not necessarily dressed in the latest trends, seasonal colour or sporting the 'happening' hairdo of the moment. It's what they do with what they have that makes them stand out – their creative combination of colours, fabrics and accessories that imparts a certain '*je ne sais quoi*'. You might not quite be able to put your finger on it, but you know they've got it.

The popular fashion magazines of the day – *Vogue, Elle, Harper's Bazaar* – would have us believe that they are the 'Holy Grails' of fashion, that they have the insider's view on 'what's in and what's not', what's 'cool' and what's not. Moreover, they subtly disseminate the message that to achieve the latest looks, you must buy their magazines and the products they promote – the *Leboutin* shoes, the *Balenciago* bag and the *Cartier* jewels. They are selling you an image, typically endorsed by a celebrity, and feeding you a lifestyle which you usually can't afford.

The question is – how can you ever develop your own style of self-presentation if you're busy trying to look like someone else? They fuel the green-eyed monster – *envy*. **Wanting to look and dress like someone else is a subtle form of envy masquerading as admiration.** In our image-conscious culture, where bold, bright and beautiful images abound at every turn (newsstands, billboards and magazine pages), nothing is left to the imagination. In fashion terms, when a dress is said to leave nothing to the imagination, it means that what is precious and ought to be protected – those more intimate parts of the human body - are exposed. Just as the soul is clothed so that none can see into it uninvited, except God, there are certain parts of the human being that are best kept private. **God has given each person an imagination to spark and nurture the vision God has placed in each heart.** The fashion industry is in danger of stealing this vision because it pigeonholes people in to fashion categories, and smothers our imaginations with external images which end up being prescriptive rather than descriptive. We are led to believe we must conform to fashion and lifestyle norms rather than dancing to a different beat – the beat of our own hearts. Indeed, images of others masquerading in the accoutrements of worldly success – the clothes, car, house and the perfect spouse and children – will never help us discover our own 'promised land'.

Current fashions are typically promoted by the ultra-thin, rich, glamorous and famous. Are you tempted to buy the latest celebrity fragrance because you like it and it smells good on you, or rather because it bolsters your self-esteem by enabling you to boast about the name, and indulge in the self-delusion that it will confer on you the qualities you believe you lack which that celebrity has in abundance. Most of the stick-thin models who parade in the clothing fashions look morose and self-conscious. The average human being on the street does not exude such an attitude. Fashion-consciousness has the potential to confer a sense of superiority. Nevertheless, looking better than someone does not make you better. **The image you project often bears little resemblance to**

the truth of your inner being. But fashion doesn't care about your interior world, whether physical or emotional. As long as you look good, who cares that you are infesting your lungs with poisonous nicotine, damaging your liver with excess alcohol or crying inside because your heart is broken!

If you feel you must dress a certain way, subscribe to a certain type of fashion, fit into a certain group or circle, there is a likelihood you're using fashion to mask your true self. Fashion can never convey the truth of peoples' identities, only perhaps their need or lack of need, to be accepted. Many would argue that fashion ought not to be taken so seriously. If that is the case, then why is the fashion industry so lucrative? No doubt, because so many of us have bought into the lies it so glamorously spins.

Chapter 3

Sexual Bondage

Sex is still fraught with taboo and controversy despite attempts to popularise and normalise it. Sex is now associated with so many perverted images that we struggle to view it in its original sense as 'love-making'. This mindset keeps us in bondage. The boundaries of acceptable sex seemed to have been extended beyond what would be considered safe, healthy or desirable.

Stolen Childhood

Increasingly young girls are being viewed as sex objects by the media and advertising industries. A BBC news report proclaimed that "Sexualisation 'harms' young girls". Examples of such sexualisation were listed – "young pop stars dressed as sex objects, dolls aimed at young girls with sexual clothing such as fishnet tights". Reference was made to an ad featuring Christina Aguilera dressed as a schoolgirl with her shirt unbuttoned, licking a lollipop. **Sexualisation occurs when a person is portrayed as having value only in relation to her or his sexual appeal or behaviour to the exclusion of other characteristics.** It was shown to harm the normal development of young girls and affect their level of confidence with their bodies, with the likelihood of depression. Dr. Zurbriggen, chair of the task force set up by the American Psychological Association, recommended replacing "these sexualised images with positive ones showing girls in positive settings"[39].

Overt sexual messages are being broadcast in the lyrics of popular mainstream music. The beat is so catchy that innocent listeners are oblivious to the words until they have been captivated by the tune. By then it is too late as it reverberates over and over in their heads de-sensitising them to its meaning. Psychologist Linda Papadopoulos has expressed concern that the explicitness of messages in mainstream music leaves nothing to the imagination. What is staggering is that so many music videos feature scantily clad women who seem oblivious to the fact that they have become caricatures of the male fantasy and are just used as *eye candy* – "they don't sing or play an instrument."[40] This is a very disempowering example for young girls and will tend to re-inforce chauvinism in young boys. Papadopoulos reckons that music carries far greater influence than the images alone – "with their drip, drip effect, song lyrics form the content to children's lives. and the effect is deeply disturbing." The crux of this effect is that children aspire to imitate in fashion, behaviour and speech, the celebrities who sing these songs or the lifestyles portrayed in the songs themselves. Furthermore, the *American Journal of Preventive Medicine* has seen a direct link between the lyrics teens listen to and their sexual behaviour. The more degrading the lyrics, the more likely teens are to become sexual at a younger age, have more sexual partners, poor sexual health and teenage pregnancy.

The *Baptist Times* featured an article publicising the imminent campaign by the Mother's Union to encourage couples to have an AIDS test before marriage. Many, like myself, will have fallen prey to the messages of the sexual revolution and have experimented with sex prior to marriage. Gone are the days when the bride and groom are virgins or keep themselves for one another after their exchange of vows. Abstinence before marriage is not a popular message and so most people do not regard it as a feasible option. My husband and I made a conscious decision to commit to sexual purity while we courted. It has helped us to treasure our marriage as the sacred and precious union that it is. Despite the myriad temptations, it is always possible to overcome them if you make a pre-determined effort to live in this world and yet not embrace its worldly mentality.[41]

From the core message that sex with anyone was fine as long as we use contraception, an even more insidious message has been spawned. The message is that we are sexual beings, first and foremost. The mass media in particular have colluded to ensure that if we are not having it, we ought to be thinking about it. It's on billboards selling underwear on nubile, young flesh, TV ads where sexual innuendo sells everything from crisps to cars, daily tabloid newspapers featuring page three models and celebrities in all stages of undress.

Remember the Liz Hurley Gucci dress – it set the tone for the belief that flesh is the new trend in fashion-consciousness. Indeed, the skin has become a fashion label to be worn as a badge of self-confidence. Chic clothes are being designed to expose the flesh so that if you are intent on being the embodiment of trendiness you will have no choice but to succumb to maximum exposure. It seems just a short while ago that Hurley grabbed the headlines with her 'safety pin' dress. Now this peek-a-boo ensemble would seem tame because a hint of sexuality has now given way to overt, unashamed immodesty. The difference between previous eras of conservative dressing and behaviour and our present age of unabashed exposure is a depreciation of the moral values of self-restraint and modesty. The popular ethos is that 'if you've got it, flaunt it!' and let's face it, we all have something. This is perfectly embodied in the TV programme *How To Look Good Naked*. The physique used to be viewed as a vessel of shame unless you happened to have a model figure, but this show suggests that body confidence can only be attained by the ultimate act of exposure– public nudity. But, freedom and self-restraint must always co-exist if anarchy is not to rule and if we are to make the most of the lives God has given us. **If there are no limits to what we will do, then there will be no limit to the chaos we will create**. Indeed, the daily news demonstrates the varieties of chaos we have created.

It was once drummed into women from an early age that they should cover up in case they are misunderstood or violated. Not any more - the 11 year old beauty queen has lowered the bar on the acceptable age to be ogled. To make matters worse, clothes have come to represent more than just necessary covering - they have become a fashion statement - an indicator of what's stylish and what's not, whose cool and whose not.

Running For Spiritual Cover

We wouldn't dream of leaving the house without our external garb. In fact, we go out of our way to purchase and dress ourselves in the clothes that we feel complement us or best reflect our personalities and taste. Similarly, we pay attention to other aspects of our appearance such as hairstyle, makeup, perfume and fresh breath. We go to such lengths to fine-tune our appearance because we are keenly aware that people judge us by this standard. We are motivated, not just from fear of catching a chill, but fear of ridicule and embarrassment.

As followers of Christ, it is even more important that we concern ourselves with another type of clothing – our spiritual clothing. If we fail to leave our homes without spiritual clothing, we are likely to bring into disrepute the person whom we represent

– Christ himself. It has happened to me on several occasions. Sleeping through my alarm clock, waking up late in a panic and skipping over my usual morning prayer, Bible study and meditation, I've nevertheless never omitted to brush my teeth. And as for styling my hair and applying makeup, well, that's a must. After all, I wouldn't want to scare the neighbours! So goes my flawed reasoning. But within minutes of stepping through the door, my state of spiritual undress betrays itself. A taxi driver runs a red light and nearly crashes into my car. I mutter an expletive under my breath. "Oops! Sorry, Lord," I mutter. The friend whom I'm supposed to meet is half an hour late for our rendezvous, thus derailing my perfectly-crafted schedule for the rest of the day. During the waiting period, I begin to think of all the reasons I should never have formed the friendship in the first place. Precisely 28 minutes and 35 seconds later I've convinced myself I've made an appointment with the devil himself, and as I'm about to speed away to the other end of town, I suddenly glimpse my friend approaching. Phew, she's only human after all! On the way home, I stop to post a letter. As I'm walking towards the post office, I pass a beggar on the street with outstretched hands and a plaintive look. I clutch my handbag, and throw him a nasty look, thinking to myself that these vagabonds ought to get off their behinds and look for work. As I walk past, a burst of wind sends my hat flying. It comes to rest within metres of the sedentary beggar. Next to him is a dog and a white stick. He's blind! Immediately a passage of the Bible comes to mind "Judge not that ye be not judged!" "Oops, sorry Lord." I decide to put on some spiritual clothing right there and then before getting home, so I reach for my Bible on the back seat. Perhaps if we determine to cultivate the true image of ourselves (the image God sees), we will spend more time developing our character than adorning our façades and massaging our egos.

Pornography

Jeannette Kupfermann fears that pornography is taking over British culture. She argues that "pornography has infiltrated mainstream culture to the extent that there is scarcely an image, entertainment, fashion or advertisement untouched by it." She points to the mainstream culture pandering to this pornographic style to sell fashions or magazines. Specific reference was made to West Yorkshire billboards promoting Harvey Nichols through the unnerving image of model Jodie Kidd in a dog collar with the ironic slogan "Harvey Nichols Leeds". This is shock advertising geared to a public that is no longer easily shocked. There were undertones of sado-masochism and enslavement which are demeaning to woman. Pornography demeans woman and the men who take part in it. It is the depiction of women as whores, objects or fetishes for the sexual titillation of others. If that titillation is used to sell a product, it doesn't make it any less pornographic. She wisely discerns that "advertisements do not exist in a moral vacuum."[42] Perhaps the biggest deception of all is that they feed all kinds of sexual fantasies which seemingly will have no bearing whatsoever on our personal lives because they appear to be harmless business strategies or just plain fun. Yet, these pornographic images rob women of a wholesome sense of self and diminish men's respect for women.

Gender Conflict

In the world, gender distinctions are emphasised in so many ways. It is shocking how little things have changed despite how far we thought we had come. The thrust of feminism was social and political equality, yet the genders do not relate to one another as equals. **Women fell into the trap of believing that equality would derive from changing the external *status quo* when, in reality, it emanates from a change of consciousness.** If we truly had this consciousness, men and women could form wholesome friendships with one another without sexual innuendo or game-playing, just as brothers and sisters generally do. There would be fewer ill-fated, unsuitable marriages, less sexual craving for Mr. or Miss Right, and less loneliness. In short, people would be fulfilled whether they're married or not. Rather what we are experiencing in the world is men and women in constant conflict and misunderstanding, men being drawn to men sexually or women being drawn to women sexually because of unfulfilled needs of the soul stemming from childhood deprivation, past abuse or a lack of positive, convincing role models of marriage in their childhood and society at large. We have a situation where people are seeking to change their gender by medical means because being their birth gender has seemingly disappointed them. Because people are being told that they are first and foremost sexual beings, with a right to explore their sexuality, the boundaries of sexual experimentation and behaviour have all but disappeared.

You may ask why God made different genders. Most agree on the functional uniqueness of being male and female for the purpose of combining strengths and weaknesses as a balanced foundation for raising a family. This is necessary for order and effectiveness. **Sex was never meant to be a free-for-all but was created to help bond a couple in the lifelong covenant of marriage and to conceive the next generation.** Sex can never cement a relationship which does not have, through the mutual understanding and commitment of both parties, the divine sanction of the holy covenant of marriage. I'm of the firm belief that many marriages which occur may have societal or legal recognition but lack the divine blessing simply because they were embarked upon in ignorance as to the deeper meaning of marriage. One of the end-time signs of social decay prior to Jesus' return is that people will be "giving themselves in marriage" which suggests that multiple marriages over a lifetime will increase because of the prevalence of divorce, polygamy and polyandry. It may also point to the increasing demand of the homosexual lobby for the right to 'marry' which seems to dominate news headlines at the moment.

It became clear after the poor judgement of Adam and Eve that men and women had experienced a seismic shift in their way of relating to one another. Adam's relentless need to work[43] would now compete with his wife for attention. Men would rule the roost[44] rather than the equality which women have sought to restore through the generations but only with partial success. Remember Adam and Eve had their union sanctified by God himself . It was the spiritual repercussions of their rebellion against God which would require this accountability before God and man –the hallmark of marriage ceremonies today.

Fastforward thousands of years, and men and women are still struggling with the roles they play in society and in the home. This headline brought home the bitterest of ironies – 'Househusband backlash as high-flying wives ditch men they wanted to stay at home'. Not only did these women lose respect for their men, they lost interest in sex. A divorce lawyer was quick to issue the warning that the stay-at-home husband could spell the death knell of many marriages, as she observed from her professional vantage point. She cautioned couples to think long and hard before embarking on this domestic experiment.[45] A woman's prerogative to change her mind is evidenced by the high incidence of divorces initiated by women. Fay Weldon stresses the urgency of reclaiming masculinity in order to revive the flagging self-esteem of so many men who feel emasculated and side-lined in this modern age. She terms it the 'femininisation' of society characterised by "turning our back on militarism, on toughness, on discipline, the aim is to care and nurture. Even the old stern Patriarch God is gone: rather we worship tender Mother Nature."[46]She calls for a 'masculinist' movement to be started because feminism has apparently gone too far. The women's movement has undermined family and marriage because women now relish the freedom to do whatever they want, indifferent to the repercussions on their children, men and society at large. Is it so bad for a man to open the door for a woman or insist on paying for a meal? If that will make him feel more masculine and worthwhile, why don't more modern women appreciate it? Women now overvalue work and undervalue their roles as wives and mothers in the home. They are content to farm out their maternal responsibilities to daycare facilities, nannies and husbands and feel justified in doing so because they are earning, not necessarily because they are obliged to work for financial survival but for the sheer relief of escaping domestic drudgery or to afford a particular lifestyle. Humans often press the self-destruct button in their efforts to do what seems right[47].

The Independent on Sunday ran a headline across their 'Real Life' section - 'Is marriage driving women mad?' It was revealed that whereas marriage offers emotional support to men, it can be a source of depression for women who struggle to communicate with an emotionally detached spouse. The media has boldly blown the trumpet, declaring that the traditional couple is dead, and must give way to the new couple. The implication is that the traditional marriage is no longer workable. Yet, the high divorce rate today coexists alongside a new wave of approaches to marriage which have deviated from the well-trodden path. Are the 'ten new laws of love'[48] really as new as they are claimed to be? The author's book in many ways, serves to remind us of the time-worn values we once held dear such as sexual exclusivity, mutual respect, making your spouse a priority and the art of forgiveness. Nowadays, couples are given options of the type of marriage which works for them. One Sociologist of sex identified three such types - the traditional, the 'near peers' and 'the peers' marriages[49]. The type of love needed to sustain marriage is self-giving and is found in those classic words " love suffers long and is kind; love does not envy; love does not parade itself, is not puffed up, does not behave rudely, does not seek its own, is not provoked, thinks no evil, does not rejoice in iniquity, but rejoices in the truth, bears all things, believes all things, hopes all things, endures all things. Love never fails."[50] Indeed, how can a marriage, or indeed any relationship not succeed with such qualities being consistently demonstrated? Marital breakdown causes stress, anxiety and resultant health problems whereas marriage is a buffer against stress and anxiety when life proves challenging[51]. There used to be a pride in having a spouse, one's own home and family such that every sacrifice was made to hold on to it. Now so much seems to be taken for granted.

Compatibility is not, contrary to popular opinion, the fact that two people are as alike as two peas in a pod. Rather it is ultimately the choice that two people make to co-exist harmoniously in spite of their differences. There is a tendency for those of us in search of a mate to draw up a checklist of the qualities that would define the perfect person. It never occurs to us to ask ourselves whether we are just as perfect as the person we seek. And perhaps if we feel we are so perfect, we might be sending the message to others that they are not good enough. The apostle Paul encouraged followers of Christ "not to think of yourself more highly than you ought to think, but to think with sober judgement."[52] In short, we can only benefit from taking the time to develop those qualities which we seek in another. On the other hand, so often we expect behaviour from others which they have given no former evidence that they can deliver. Let's say I appoint you to the position of 'perfect, will-always -be- there-for-me' human being. Wow, what a compliment! But, surprisingly,

I forgot to notify you of this summary appointment, so you just kept on behaving as you normally would. Result - my disappointment in you. If you had been informed, you would have had the right to reply "Sorry, I'm flattered, but this new role is too big to fill. You'll have to find someone else or better yet, get real." A disappointment is a disillusionment, but it is we who create the illusions in the first place. After all, the best of a human being is still at best a human being. The Bible reminds us constantly that "there is no-one who is righteous, not even one..."[53]

Promiscuity

Where does sexual promiscuity begin? It starts with the eyes feeding the imagination and the imagination running rampant. The imagination is made up of more images than sounds, thanks in no small measure to TV and image-based broadcasting. When a strong enough image forms in the mind, it can create desires which would not otherwise have developed. And of course, the more images we are exposed to, the stronger the desire becomes. Why, for example, do we see ourselves today primarily as sex objects and not just physiological beings? After all, the reality of the body is undeniable, but why do we persistently focus on the aspects associated specifically with sex to the extent that the whole body has come to be associated with sex? This sexual-obsessiveness, whereby even the hint or suggestion of sex is used to sell unrelated products like toilet tissue or beverages, explains the rise of paedophilia, incidences of doctors having sex with patients under anaesthesia, and even highly-esteemed men of God becoming engaged in pornography or fornication. Pre-occupation with sex is fostered in nearly all sectors of society, and it requires a great deal of strength to resist.

Sex has now become a source of danger and scandal because its original use has been perverted. It was intended to be a covenantal seal on the marriage union, a shared pleasure between husband and wife to remind them of their covenant promises and which would help them overcome all the stresses the marital union was bound to face. It is in this secure environment that children were to be brought into the world. Our failure to appreciate and honour sex as the sacred act it was designed to be also brings physical repercussions. In Britain, the number of sexually transmitted infections (STI's) has doubled in five years, and many people are unable to be treated promptly or at all[54]. A recent report confirms that there were 500,000 new cases of STIs in 2009.[55]

The feel-good factor which sex promises has been portrayed as a feeling worth chasing for its own sake. The orgasm is a heightened state of vulnerability which leaves both genders literally shaking, having given themselves completely to one another. The soul comprises one's emotions, intellect and will. At that moment all three are surrendered, leaving both parties wide open to hurt and exploitation. Men can be emotionally hurt just as women can, and so too can prostitutes, rapists and paedophiles. **Any perversion of the true purpose of the sex act causes untold damage to peoples' souls and bodies.** Many view the prospect of sex with fear, dread or apathy because of past sexual misuses and abuses.

The sexual revolution has conferred on women the same rights as men in the area of sexual behaviour. They can prey on men and engage in promiscuity to the degree that any man would. Angela Lambert recognises this behaviour as a betrayal of the hard-fought female cause for gender equality. She states "women struggled and suffered, were imprisoned and force-fed, marched and demonstrated, were beaten up and mocked, to win the vote and give freedom to generations as yet unborn...It is a cynical betrayal for the newly-liberated to misuse that freedom only to behave like the vilest of men."[56]

Sex was not designed for entertainment or as a pastime. We have reverted to the purely animalistic behaviour whereby sex has no value apart from the act itself. This mentality is promoted in popular television programmes such as *Sex and the City* and *Desperate Housewives*. **Sex was intended to be part of a continuum of intimacy not a brief act of lustful gratification with a stranger or friend.**

Has modern society spawned a generation of young women who pop 'morning- after pills' like candy with no measurable impact on their desire to re-evaluate their sexual behaviour? 23 Studies from around the world reveal that morning- after pills do not reduce pregnancy or abortion rates[57] . In the UK the morning-after pill is available without prescription from pharmacies. For women casual sex was never going to be an easy option – a universal myth spawned by the women's liberation movement. A woman's sexual behaviour has repercussions on her health, fertility and happiness for the duration of her life, way beyond the fleeting moment of sexual excitement.

Body Distortion

When we recognise the value of the human body and the damage we can wreak on others through our own selfish need for sexual gratification, we will in turn begin to appreciate the values of self-restraint and modesty. When Adam strayed from God's Way, he sought to cover up his nakedness. It's as if he knew instantly the evil of which his body was now capable and to which it was now vulnerable. His nudity was not a problem beforehand because he was only aware of God's will for his body. It's not the body itself which is the problem but how it is portrayed and hence perceived. A woman who is giving birth in a state of exposure or breastfeeding will create minimum fuss or attention, but put that same woman in a seductive pose and she is suddenly a threat to male restraint, other women's sense of security and a model for other impressionable women to emulate. The image of women posing and pouting suggestively is now so universal in Western society that men have a tendency to carry this mindset wherever they go, and transpose this image on nude or sparsely-dressed women they see in reality, regardless of the age of the female or the context of her appearance.

In human terms, the body is seen as our greatest asset but not from the point of view of doing good or bestowing service such as hands that feed the hungry, eyes that shed tears of compassion or mouths that utter words of encouragement and consolation. Unfortunately, it has come to be viewed as a display-piece to be flaunted to impress or as an object for the gratification of others.

Romantic Delusions

The movie and romantic fiction industries thrive on this ideal – that there is someone special out there just for us who will accept us as we are, to mirror our thoughts and hopes and aspirations. Without such a person, we tell ourselves, our lives are doomed to a miserable, lonely, unfulfilled existence. The suffering that we cause ourselves as a result of this philosophy is immeasurable. We don't have the confidence to do things which society tells us are reserved for two, but which deep down we would love to try such as travelling or going to the cinema alone. And as for showing up at a dinner party or wedding alone, that would be unheard of. If we think of someone as our 'significant other', does that mean that the others (whether they be parents, friends, siblings or children) are any less significant**? And if this 'significant other' were to decide to have a fling, disappear in the middle of the night or file for divorce, would our lives be any less significant?** In her tantalising article - "Can too much intimacy destroy true love?"[58] Virginia Ironside questions whether it has been destructive to marriage to look to it as the "principal source of happiness." She reckons that this heightened expectation has led to the devaluation of the surpassing virtues of kindness, loyalty and trust which we can show to and receive from people in general, not just our spouses.

Why do we desire this special someone so much? Could it be that we long to escape from a difficult reality – demanding parents, an unfulfilling job or our own shyness in public? We expect this person to turn up on the scene and make it all better – to, in effect, be our crutch. This person no doubt holds the same expectations of us. So two people come together with unrealistic expectations – a recipe for disaster and disappointment. The author of *Women Who Love Too Much*, is a self-confessed recovered relationship addict. She used to be drawn to men who mistreated her and for whom nothing she did was ever good enough. Yet she put up with it for too long because she was addicted to love. Her advice to other women like her is to put yourself first instead of last.[59] Perhaps the answer is rather that we must put God first since He alone is the embodiment of perfect love. **When we rely on another human being to fill up our love tank, we use love as an exhausting barter to get our needs met.** The question becomes not who can I extend myself in love towards because God's love has been poured out abundantly in my heart, but rather what do I have to give up today to be loved? Many trade in their bodies and dignity only to receive the crumbs of pseudo-acceptance and approval.

Chapter 4

Verbal Diarrhoea

The Force Of Words

The world's culture teaches us that words are of no lasting value. As such we toss them about casually in relationships to make a point or get a laugh. Nowadays the trend is to say whatever comes to mind, and we fail to realise that we are sowing seeds into the future. Many just speak to release themselves of pent-up emotions because they don't know how to pause and reflect or pray. They are unaware that **while emotions are temporary, words have long-term effects.** Praying is pro-active and it seeks a solution as opposed to indulging in mere self-pity.

Since it is what comes out of a peoples' hearts and mouths through words which pollute them rather than what goes into their mouths[60], it would appear that our culture has its emphasis totally wrong. In Western nations where food is in relative abundance, many are obsessed with restricting their food intake so they can keep slim and trim. There are probably more diets than human languages. It has never occurred to us that we should go on a verbal diet. Just as the more calories we consume, the heavier we will be, the more we speak, the more we offend.[61]

The tongue may be compared to a fire - only a few words can kindle a forest fire which causes untold damage. Blessings and curses did not originally refer to material gain or lack but words spoken over people which either healed or harmed, prospered or punished. Disciples of Christ are enjoined to bless and not curse their enemies – gracious gestures which require supernatural self-restraint to accomplish. Indeed, words even have the power to affect our health. The more anger and bitterness we express, the more likely we are to have high blood pressure which in turn puts our physical hearts at risk.

Verbal Renewal Plan

The book of Proverbs offer wisdom for everyday living. It consists of 31 chapters which equates to the total number of days in most months. Each chapter contains insights on the potential of words to cause good or evil.

Day/Chapter 1

"If sinners entice you, do not consent"

Verse 10 highlights the need to say 'no' when we are tempted to join ranks with evil men in the pursuit of evil ends. It could be even learning to say 'no' to time-wasting activities. Our decision-making is invariably connected with our value system. Failure to honour this relationship of values and choice leads to a guilty conscience. For example, if we value being slim and healthy yet continue to choose junk food over sound nutrition, then we are contradicting our desires and our choices are belying our values. Evil is not always obvious, but think whether the end result is profitable.

Day/chapter 2

"[she] who flatters with her words"

Verse 16 addresses the seductive words of the wayward wife or adulteress. In general terms, it illustrates the dangers of flattery. There is always an agenda behind false, unmerited or excessive compliments. Be aware of the danger signs when you are tempted to flatter to get something you want such as approval or favour, and when you are on the receiving end of flattery because it is always the case that some form of manipulation is being tried and tested.

Day/chapter 3

"Do not say to your neighbour, "go and come back, and tomorrow I will give it," when you have it with you.

Verse 28 reveals the lack of integrity in procrastinating with a promise. Our words are not just what we say but who we are. If our deeds align with our words, we develop a reputation for honour and reliability.

Day/chapter 4

"put away from you a deceitful mouth"

It is clear from verse 24 that truthfulness should not be reserved for giving a testimony in court when one is required to swear to tell 'the whole truth and nothing but the truth'. Truth starts with recognising our natural bent towards all manner of deception – we wear masks, we speak euphemisms, we indulge in denial – all to avoid the truth. At the root of this is our sinful nature, and its antidote is found in finding our way back to God through Jesus' remission of our sins, and the Holy Spirit's transformation of our sinful natures. It starts by saying 'yes' to God's masterplan for saving humanity.

Day/chapter 5

"I have not obeyed the voice of my teachers"

Our teachers may come in different guises and with different messages. God sent Mordecai to lead Esther to her calling[62], Samuel to warn Saul against taking a wrong path[63] and Philip to explain truths to the Ethiopian.[64] Who in your life so far have played these roles for you?

Day/chapter 6

Verses 1-6 warns us against making dangerous promises where we stand to lose more than we can afford if we fail to make good on the promise. The 2008 global financial recession was due in part to sub-prime mortgages where people were allowed to buy homes they could not afford. Whether or not we can afford something may involve calculations of time, relationships and peace of mind as well as money.

Day/chapter 7

Verse 11 states that the loose woman *is "loud and wayward."* Those who are persistently loud desire to call attention to themselves. It is sometimes difficult to avoid loud people but we instinctively baulk at their words because they are vexatious to the spirit. More impact is often caused by quiet words than loud ones.

Day/chapter 8

Wisdom has a voice and she beckons to all to listen. What accrues to those who find her are justice, riches, honour and righteousness.

Day/chapter 9

Rebuke and correction must be delivered with discretion. A scoffer will hate you for it, while a wise man will love you for it.

Day/chapter 10

Many metaphors are used to describe the speech of a righteous person. Verse 11 states that *"the mouth of the righteous is a well of life"* while verse declares that *"the tongue of the righteous is choice silver"*. Furthermore, *"the lips of the righteous know what is acceptable"*[65]

Day/chapter 11

A gossip or tale-bearer (verse 13) is to be avoided at all costs because he reveals secrets. Whenever we are about to talk about someone else, we should ask ourselves whether the person would appreciate being discussed in that way. If the answer is 'no' or there is any doubt, then desist.

Day/chapter 12

We are told that *"counsellors of peace have joy."* To be a peacemaker is to sow seeds of peace with your words.

Day/chapter 13

Choosing your words carefully can determine your longevity (verse 3).

Day/chapter 14

A fool speaks loud boasts of pride (verse 3). Proverbial wisdom teaches that pride comes before destruction.

Day/chapter 15

A soft answer has the effect of pacifying anger. Many a full-blown escalation of hostilities, whether personal or national, could have been averted through a gentle response.

Day/chapter 16

Verse 25 – Speaking pleasant words has psychological and physical benefits.

Day/chapter 17

God judges harshly those who make fun of the poor (verse 5) which it is all too easy to do in our hearts when we confront homeless people on the street. We may ignore them or toss a bit of loose change in their direction to palliate our consciences, but deep down we hold them in contempt.

Day/chapter 18

Verse 13 highlights the need for good listening and deliberation before responding appropriately to any matter.

Day/chapter 19

The false witness cannot escape punishment. Although the human judge may not detect or punish his falsehood, the day of reckoning cannot be escaped by the ultimate Judge himself.

Day/chapter 20

A stern warning is made against cursing one's parents. This may well have been the cause of many premature deaths. This of course refers to children and parents of any age. The biblical injunction to honour one's parents lasts as long as they are alive. It is evident in the fifth commandment and is unique among the 10 commandments as it is the only one that comes with a bonus for obedience – *"honour your father and your mother... that it may go well with you and that you may enjoy long life on the earth."*[66]

Day/chapter 21

Verse 19 invites every nagging wife to take heed as husbands often take extreme measures to distance themselves from her irritating words. To foster harmony in the home means that wives must choose the outlet of prayer rather than nagging.

Day/chapter 22

Verse 13 suggests that a lazy person is known more by his words than his passivity. He uses excuses and unfounded fears to justify his complacency.

Day/chapter 23

Our words must be selected not just for their life-promoting value, but we must choose our words depending on the hearers who are present. Wise words should not, for example, be wasted on fools (verse 9).

Day/chapter 24

We are cautioned against speaking words of vengeance in verse 29. God has re-assured His children that "*vengeance is mine.*" We must be patient in waiting for God's perfect justice to be dispensed.

Day/chapter 25

Verse 23 reveals that the words we speak shape our countenance. It is impossible to say angry words with a calm demeanour and vice versa. As we age, we all get the faces we deserve which reflect the inner lives we have led and the emotions we have harboured.

Day/chapter 26

Verse 19 discourages deception under the guise of joking. Irony is a device used frequently to make critical or nasty comments without the listener knowing.

Day/chapter 27

We should never boast about our plans as we don't know what the future holds(verse 1). We must entrust our plans to god who orders our footsteps, and although we do not know what the future holds, we know that He holds the future.

Day/chapter 28

Verse 13 demonstrates the benefit of confessing ones sins. Sometimes we need to confess to God alone, sometimes also to others whom we have wronged.

Day/chapter 29

Verse 11 shows the folly of saying exactly what comes into one's head immediately and without any restraint.

Day/chapter 30

We should let other people praise us and not seek to exalt ourselves with our own lips (verse 32).

Day/chapter 31

Verse 26 states that the virtuous wife "speaks with wisdom." Wisdom is the ability to apply knowledge and judgement appropriately to a given situation. Wisdom is its own reward. We are told that *"long life is in her right hand; in her left hand are riches and honour. Her ways are pleasant ways, and all her paths are peace.*"[67]

Everyday Verbal Assaults

The simple act of shopping for food or clothing will necessitate entering a shop where secular music is perceptible from the loudspeaker. The tempo and tone of the music is designed to keep you in the shop for as long as possible so you will buy more. The assault is therefore on your mind as well as your wallet both in the most subtle fashion. You might be seduced by the lyric "If it makes you happy, it can't be that bad" sung by Sheryl Crow in such a soothing way that you reckon a bit of retail therapy is justified. So the credit card gets an extra, unplanned battering. Caught up in the frenetic rush to shop until you drop, you don't even think twice about the lyric. This tune is advocating a "what the heck, anything goes" libertarian outlook on life. It runs counter to Christ-like thinking, but you think nothing of it because it's only in the background. It's not as if you spent money to buy the song. This is where we allow complacency to set in.

Elusive Silence

Perhaps the strongest urge we humans experience apart from hunger is the urge to speak even when what we have to say is of little or no benefit to us or anyone else for that matter. Speaking for the sake of speaking is endemic. If we appreciated the fact that when we speak, we're writing the script for our lives, we would adhere to the exhortation to be "quick to listen, slow to speak."[68] The individual's right to silence extends beyond the boundaries of a courtroom. In our everyday lives, we must rely on this right if we are not to divulge confidences or personal information about ourselves to those who may use it against us. The Bible cautions that "The mouths of fools are their ruin, and their lips a snare to themselves."[69] The real challenge of telling the truth arises where information is requested that we would not have volunteered. For instance, how do we deal with the nosey questioning from an acquaintance or complete stranger about our financial income? It would be oh so easy to employ the so-called harmless 'white lie' when another alternative could be to steer the conversation in a different direction. We often fear embarrassing others so much that we fail to appreciate that being truthful about how much we are comfortable revealing about ourselves to others can only lay the foundation for an honest relationship where people know where we stand.

It doesn't help that our culture encourages venting or blabbing. "Get it off your chest!" Psychotherapists advocate. "It's good to talk" is the popular British Telecom slogan. The Americans have invented the modern phenomenon of the 'talk show' where people are encouraged to vent their spleens for the purpose of entertainment. It's more like a salacious attempt to garner fifteen minutes of fame. The Jerry Springer show is a modern example of people unleashing their every thought and emotion on public television due to a lack of self-restraint and moral integrity. Every support service available runs a group so people with similar problems and concerns can air their views with the security of knowing that they will not be told to shut up. In America, even the wealthy have groups to share the agonies of having too much money and too little wisdom to know what to do with it.

Jesus wanted to save us from this 'blab' trap. He knew the significance of words, even idle ones. Just as His Father had spoken words to frame creation, we have the ability (because we are made in God's image), to create life or death with our tongues. **We speak as if our lives depend on it not realising that they do.**[70] It seems that we're speaking more death than life over ourselves and each other. Look around you and you'll see the fruit of our lips. Each winter predictions are made of how many senior citizens will succumb to the cold. This causes fear and anxiety in the hearts of our precious golden oldies who become paralysed by fear, do nothing to safeguard their health and consequently cause these predictions to become self-fulfilling. Words can even influence our health, with pleasant words having the capacity to bring healing to the bones.[71]

Where speaking is concerned, more damage has been done in jest than in seriousness. Notice the figures of speech – 'break a leg', 'I'm cracking up', 'you're as mad as a hatter', 'I'm bored to tears'. Even the prefix 'bloody' takes blood for granted. God considers 'blood' as sacred and the shedding of blood a very serious matter. He allowed His Son to shed his blood for the sins of mankind, and the murderous shedding of another man's blood brings a terrible curse.[72] The culture has been effective in blinding us to the long-term significance of careless words spoken over and over again to rob them of their true meaning.

When Jesus was challenged regarding the woman caught in adultery, he paused and wrote in the sand. This is significant because he could easily have been provoked to angry words. How many of us are pausing before we speak, particularly, when we feel anger rising up within us? The New Testament book of James tells us that the tongue is "a world of iniquity", and that it is the hardest part of the body to tame even though it is one of the smallest.[73]

Lost In Music

How do you remember your life? You may have a photographic memory, in which case you're one of the fortunate few, but in all probability it's through photographs, letters, verbal recollections passed down from family and certain things people told you or you told yourself. How many have said "I will never..." as a shout or a mumble? Are you still struggling to live down those statements today? Music is another memory tool. Whenever I hear a familiar old tune, it brings me back to a moment in time with pin-point accuracy and the words of the song and the feelings they evoked come flooding back. That's why I'm very careful about the words that I listen to and sing especially soul music and love songs. They were my favourite genre for many years because I considered myself a romantic, reflective soul. But have you noticed that these songs are predominantly about heartbreak, loneliness and rejection? Well, when I finally got convicted of that revelation, I made up my mind to get rid of most of my soul music and replace them with songs which would edify my soul instead of leaving it dejected.

When I first moved into my husband's house after we got married, he had an impressively-sized collection of CDs screaming "play me" every time I entered the lounge. His collection spanned about six decades from the forties. I was intrigued, but on closer inspection, I became a bit concerned. Just the titles of the tracks unnerved me. Not that they were overtly risqué but I was on a spiritual journey which had sharpened my antennae for potential pollutants. As for my husband, he had long forgotten about his CDs which were gathering dust. He didn't have the sensitivity to music that I had, and could hardly even remember the words of one lyric let alone hundreds. I, on the other hand, had only to hear the first line of a lyric playing in a shop and I would be able to sing along. As a child, music had been my refuge. Now it was a stronghold I sought to dismantle.

It wasn't until our second anniversary that I plucked up the courage to inform my husband that I was going to downsize our collection to make way for more Christian and wholesome music. With his blessing, I managed to remove 55 CDs from the shelves. I became aware that there were four aspects of a song to consider – the title, the lyrics, the way the song is arranged and the way it is actually sung. I truly believe, for example, that a depressed person could sing an uplifting song in such a way that the spirit of depression is transferred through that song. Here are some examples of songs which did not quit fit the criteria:

Michael Bolton's 'Yesterday': There's nothing hopeful about a lyric which says "I believe in yesterday." Also, "Knock on wood" is nothing but superstition.

Shania Twain: 'Don't be Stupid' and 'That don't impress me much' suggest game-playing in relationships which on the surface may seem like fun but actually causes a lot of unhappiness.

The Best of James Bond: This compilation of theme music from the films brought flashbacks of scenes of sexual dalliances and violence from what is popularly considered family fun.

Phil Collins: "I don't care anymore" – if you repeat that enough times, you might not care about anything.

Rita Coolidge: 'I'd rather leave when I'm in love' – a song about sabotaging a relationship for fear it won't last. What could be more heart-breaking.

Most of these songs seemed harmless enough judging by the titles, but they failed to inspire. Some were famous names that had faded into oblivion. They reminded me of the temporal nature of fame, and that I must not allow my musical preferences to be dictated by what's trendy. A lot of the music was like postcards which took me back to times of my life when purity had not been a priority, when I was in places or with people I ought not to have been with. To this day I cannot listen to Natalie Cole's 'Miss you like crazy' without the pain of my long-distance romance. It is therefore not a song I would choose to keep in my collection, and if it came on the radio, I would immediately switch it off. I recall the summer of 1999 when the song with the racy lyrics reverberated across the airwaves - 'a little bit of Monica in my life, a little bit of Erica by my side...' It was the summer I decided to buy my son a karaoke machine. The sample tape featured that song – it made fooling around and being a 'Casanova' seem like fun. I'm sure most fans were willing to overlook that because it was such a catchy tune. Such tunes can be repeated in our minds for years, even decades, subconsciously influencing our behaviour.

Most love songs are overly-sentimental, focus on yearning for a lost love, forbidden love or a fantasy of love. Most of it is not love at all but lust, heartache and heart-break. Overall the picture painted of love is distorted and painful. The music industry has spun a rhythmic deception. Is art imitating life or life imitating art?

There's a fine line between simple entertainment and the dissemination of subliminal messages through music. A University of Pittsburgh study found that a third of popular music contains drug references.[74] We may think we are merely being entertained, but the more we listen to music with less than wholesome lyrics, and watch the videos which interpret these lyrics, our moral radar is being de-sensitised to accept as normal the behaviour being portrayed. In the brazen world of make-believe, we like to believe anything goes, that words can be tossed around recklessly or creatively for effect. The use of the word 'bitch' in many modern music lyrics has the potential to shape the way men see women and women see themselves. We tend to get seduced by the beat of a snappy tune without thinking much about the lyrics. Many lyrics are barely audible and the shocking truth is we could be singing about anything. The spirit behind the song or the attitude or mood in which the song was arranged or performed makes a big difference. That's why some classical music leaves us melancholy and others leave us on cloud nine.

Telling Tales

Gossiping strikes at the heart of truth-telling. Information about others becomes distorted when it is tossed back and forth like a basketball. Gossip is any kind of discussion about others in their absence that you would not dare tell them to their face. The word has become sanitised in our modern-day culture, thanks in part to television dramas such as *Gossip Girl* and the band name *Gossip*. Perhaps the antidote to gossiping lies in feeling free to say to someone on the prowl for some juicy news - "I think others should have the right to convey that information about themselves." We must resist being bullied into divulging confidential or intimate information about others to third parties who are curious. Magazines, newspapers and internet sites abound which claim to provide ongoing coverage of celebrities' lives. I once got into a heated debate with a family member over coverage of a celebrity story which she had interpreted as the gospel truth. When challenged on the story's credibility, she defended the publication, which as it turned out, was a product of the 'yellow press' – a vernacular used to describe journalism which is poorly-researched and relies on scandal-mongering. Because these stories tend to have legs, they are then reproduced in several other publications when there may be little evidence of their credibility. Often a story revolves around a picture – a split-second portrayal of reality – where many assumptions and hasty conclusions are made to create a juicy story which will increase the sales of the publication. As usual, **the culture is ruled by an escapist mentality where an alternate reality is preferred to actual reality.** Why? Because reality may just be too bland for our salacious appetites. After all, it's hard to re-adjust the palate to plain cooking when you've had several years of hot and spicy cooking.

Courageous Truth-Telling

So many of us have a problem with speaking the truth because we equate it with hurting other peoples' feelings. But truth does not automatically mean tactlessness or indiscretion. In a way truth has its own force and does not need to be forcefully declared to have an impact. When we speak what we claim to be the truth with an attitude of sarcasm or aggression, there is usually a hang-up or prejudice lurking behind the words. For example, if a female companion asks us how she looks and we say "terrible", there is a danger of wounding her self-esteem with such an abrupt, blanket statement which says very little about her actual appearance. A more appropriate response could be: "the colour of that dress does not bring out the best in you but your make-up is lovely." By phrasing our response in this way, not only have we given a helpful insight, but we haven't undermined her self-confidence in the process. Truth always clarifies by being, by its very nature, specific.

Indeed, life is very rarely black or white - it is awash with varying nuances of grey. What happens is that for our own convenience, we tend to generalise and use vague language so that we don't have to justify our views. After all, no-one really wants to be proven wrong. We cannot lay claims to the truth the way we hold an opinion. **The truth simply is what it is, it has a permanence and authority of its own that existed long before we perceived it and will continue long after we've forgotten it.** When we come to grips with truth in our lives, we must be grateful to God for giving us the wisdom to recognise and understand it. Wisdom is not truth but simply the ability to discern and extract truth in any given situation. Therefore when we speak the truth, there is no need for arrogance or any sense of one-upmanship for it is God who provides the wisdom to recognise truth for what it is.

To speak the truth is often to incur the disfavour of others. Yet, the benefits of truth far outweigh its disadvantages. We can only find truth in our lives if we are honest with ourselves and others. How so, you may ask? Well, for example, how do you attract the right sort of mate if you put up a front? When that front collapses, as inevitably it must, the incompatibility of two individuals will result in a disharmonious relationship. Similarly, what's the point of lying on your CV that you're computer literate, then when you get the job you're afraid of being shown up as the phoney that you are. But, if truth-telling is so wonderful, then why are we penalised for doing so in everyday life? As a result, we give false information because we don't feel we measure up as we are. Indeed, truth-telling requires a great deal of faith. This faith inspires the conviction that, even though we may be penalised in our day-to-day affairs in the short-term, that in the overall scheme of things we will be rewarded. After all, a just God would not advocate honesty if it were not in our own best interest.

The folly of lying is that it weaves an insidious web of even more deception. It seems that once we've started, we can't stop. To save face, we continue lying even though it is strictly unnecessary. It becomes a vicious cycle until one day we are discovered or we discover for ourselves the sobering truth of how untrustworthy we have become and just how much of our lives is based on lies. **The sad truth is that when we lie to others, ironically it becomes easier to lie to ourselves.**

It is all too easy not to speak the truth for fear of repercussions. The witty saying that 'confession is good for the soul but bad for the reputation', exposes our general unwillingness to face up to the truth about ourselves. We would rather hold tenaciously to a self-image that allows others to view us positively, even though it may be based on lies, rather than relinquish it and endure the discomfort even humiliation of rebuilding a more authentic one. But disciples of Christ are encouraged to "confess their sins to one another and pray for one another"[75] as a way of keeping their consciences clear before God and man. But truth does not have to be a 'no pain, no gain' double-edged sword. **Any pain associated with the truth stems from an accompanying effort to suppress or deny it.** Ultimately, God is the author of truth, and for those who are open to it, the Bible is the gateway for all truth-seekers. [76]

Chapter 5

Media Mayhem

The media (audio, visual and print) influences our minds more than we would care to admit. We would all like to think that we're original thinkers with a mind of our own, but the sad reality is that we have all, to some extent or the other, been infiltrated by the lies and values spun by television. This twentieth century invention has done a lot of good, but like most of man's inventions, it is being used for more evil then good. As we spend more time vegetating in front of the box, we're spending less time with each other in meaningful conversation and activity. **It's no co-incidence that the breakdown of the family can be traced back to the introduction of the television into the family home.** Even more pronounced is our contentment in living out our dreams vicariously through the exploits of celebrities in their personal lives or through fictional portrayals on screen. We're being over-loaded with negative and distracting news, values and behaviour. The world has been set up to trap us into this lifestyle whereby we lose our minds in a constant barrage of 24-hour news, broadband internet connection and ipods to carry wherever we go. The question arises - in the final analysis when we appear before our creator God, will our lives be evaluated on our emotional responses to changing world events or on how we responded to the truth of God's Word?

Hardly a home in Britain, indeed the western world, is not outfitted with a television. In the UK we moan about our ever-inflating TV license, yet few of us would dare consider the alternative – life without the box. In countries where the media is not state-regulated, we have freedom of the press, thereby ensuring diversity of opinion and subject-matter. But from God's point of view, any information or imagery which does not accord with His purposes has the potential for evil. There's no grey area. This truth is hard for most people to swallow, even Christ devotees because secular society has disseminated the crafty notion that the more choices we are given, the more good choices will result. Instead, we're bombarded with more varieties of evil programming and bad news. The only option available to Christians is to vet the media with increasing vigilance. It has been observed that we can no longer rely on external vetting agencies to sanitise out viewing:

"the media has increasingly neglected its responsibility to provide people with what they need to know in order to better not only their own lives, but society as a whole, in favour of blowing up out of all proportion, the trivial, the voyeuristic and the sensational."[77]

A typical day for a Christ follower in terms of information flowing through the eye-gate and ear-gate will illustrate the need to "be sober, be vigilant."[78] Drop in to any newsagent on the way home or even a petrol station, and one of the first images to accost you will be a half-naked woman on a magazine cover. The blatantly sexual message is that women are sex objects and that sex is a thrilling pastime devoid of responsibility. This imagery is no longer reserved for the 'dirty magazines' on the top shelf; it's on the front pages of the yellow press like *the Daily Star*, and on the covers of celebrity magazines like *The Enquirer*. It's no wonder that the last frontier of bodily innocence – the naked baby – has now become sexualised as part of a growing trend of child pornography and paedophilia. We think these evil trends are reserved for the extreme end of human social depravity, but our complacent acceptance of this imagery has resulted in a spirit of lust running rampant while we do nothing.

The earnest resolve of King David not to "look on vanities"[79] still holds relevance today. How is a Christian supposed to deal with this massive, constant assault on the eyes? Men must struggle with the command not to look lustfully on a woman which is the equivalent of committing adultery with her.[80] With females, it's more insidious. Nudity does not appeal, but we're attracted to posh/trendy clothes. We're seduced more by the hip way the clothes are presented on the female body than by the clothes themselves. So no banal clothing catalogue will do, our eyes and appetites tend to stray towards the celebrity magazines and women's fashion or lifestyle magazines. We associate the clothes with the media 'stars' and believe that wearing those clothes will make us like them, even if just momentarily. We have developed an insatiable need to know what's going on inside the private lives of celebrities. Taking part in gossip, even through listening or reading, is dangerous. Reading the captions attached to the photos means we are likely to believe the publication's interpretation of the photos even if they couldn't be further from the truth.

We turn on the television to unwind in the evening oblivious to the fact that while we've removed our spiritual armour,[81]the devil is still actively sowing seeds of evil and temptation. Even if you're watching the news to know what's happening in the world (a seemingly innocuous activity), the adverts will have a corrupting influence. Advertising preys on three human factors:

- the herd instinct (we want to be like others)
- peoples' competitiveness (we want to keep up with the Joneses)
- peoples' inadequacy (we want to buy or do something to stop us feeling so bad about ourselves).

So, for example, an ad might promote a new film which is touted as a must-see for all children and a must-send by all parents. Recently, this was the case with the *Harry Potter* movies. Despite its demonic subject matter on witches and wizards, many parents fell for the advertising hard-sell that it was an educational experience for their children by encouraging them to read and expand their imaginations. Any Christ follower will struggle to find a film which does not say the Lord's name in vain. **The problem with most films is that the reality which is portrayed is an alternate one where God does not factor at all other than as a swear word or passing reference.** He is not portrayed in His true essence as the centre and creator of the universe, and as the reason we "live and move and have our being."[82] Most entertainment is therefore an escape from reality into a godless world where people act as they please with no fear of God. Most films do not fulfil the prayer of every God seeker "let your will be done on earth as it is in heaven."[83]

When the latest digital camera, mobile phone or model of a car comes out, advertisers aim to stimulate a desire to have it. Ladies' products are invariably promoted by stunning models with perfect skin and physiques. We then crave the product in an attempt to be like them, or we become so demoralised that we fall prey to the food ads to eat something to comfort our wounded self-image such as a particular brand of crisps to bring that extra pizzazz to our palates.

When someone is born into God's family, he takes all these sinful tendencies to the cross to be washed away in the atoning blood of Jesus. Nevertheless, the renewal of the mind requires a daily crucifying of these tendencies of the old nature. This means that we must make every effort to avoid activities or information associated with the old man and his way of thinking.

Many have fallen hook, line and sinker for the highly impressionistic art-form of TV. Now that it's becoming interactive, it's easy to be lulled into a sense of quasi-communication with the box. Yet, it will never be able to listen and respond in a spontaneous way. It can never replace a human being in that respect. Yet, soap operas like *Eastenders*, *Coronation Street* and *Home and Away* have become like virtual communities. **Instead of looking forward to returning home at the end of the day to have a good conversation with the spouse or neighbour, we make a date with a soap opera which has no human ability to give or receive love.**

The Notion Of Romanticism

Consider the themes of films such as get involved with a prostitute and you can end up happily ever after. Cue *Pretty Woman*! What about falling in love with your paid escort whom you have brought to your sister's wedding so you will not appear single. Cue *The Wedding Date*! These are not just improbable storylines but they infer the message that the ends justify the means. These iconic films have come to define the culture.

Mary Ellen Ashcroft observes that the New Testament endorsement of celibacy as a lifestyle which enables you to wholeheartedly dedicate yourself to serving God is not typically promoted by the church. Books by Christian writers and publishers which give guidance on how to find 'Mr. Right', are now in high demand.[84] The author equates the romantic obsession as a type of "pornography" because it distorts the reality of life and love.[85] It is observed that singleness is a natural state since we come into the world single unless we are one of a twin. It is clear that Christian women have been brainwashed since childhood by the unscriptural notion that they are incomplete without a man. As a result, many put their lives on hold, and don't make the effort to discover what God wants them to do with their lives.

The Rise Of Reality TV

How much of TV is real? Reality TV is responsible for a spew of immorality and stereotypes. The real world is not so predictable and neatly packaged. We are conditioned to accept what we see as real, or more to the point, as how life should be. But this is often very far from the truth. Most people are not interested in the lives of the humdrum and the normal, but are drawn to the lives of the posh and the privileged. Not only may this breed 'aspirational' goals which are unattainable, such as MTV cribs, but it may result in an inferiority complex whereby we look down on ourselves and our own lives which appear dull and mediocre by comparison. By contrast, perhaps we need to see other peoples' realities in their grossest excesses to feel morally superior in some way.

It has been observed that:

"Such shows frequently portray a modified and highly influenced form of reality with participants put in exotic locations or abnormal situations, sometimes coached to act in certain ways by off-screen handlers, and with events on screen sometimes manipulated through editing and other post-production techniques."[86]

Not only does TV show what is offensive or trivial but many such shots may linger on screen long enough to give the impression of importance, and to leave a lasting impression. In effect, we are manipulated, but in a subtle way which we fail to recognise often before it's too late. There's a growing tendency to shorten the length of clips in certain programmes like documentaries. The effect the equivalent of a string of snap shots. You leave the settee in a daze unable to recall any visual or audible details. This is having an obvious effect on our concentration spans, particularly those of our children. We are in danger of side-lining the experiential in favour of the virtual. Whatever we experience with our five senses enhances our capacity for future recall. These experiences create lasting memories we will treasure as we grow older. The same cannot be said of virtual experiences.

TV is the ultimate escape from reality. We were created to immerse ourselves in the tasks before us or apply ourselves to our own life challenges, not to live vicariously through others, particularly fictional characters. TV and films encourage indulgence in many emotions which ought not to be encouraged. **Why do we need to know what it feels like to see a starving child when we're in no position to embrace or feed them?** Why do we need to know what it feels like to kill someone (films try to recreate the ambiance) when we are not in a position to feel or act on our remorse. In fact most violence is depicted so clinically that we have become desensitised to what it really means to injure or kill another human being. God does not take this lightly and neither should we.

Many are lonely and feel a void because they are relying on imaginary characters to keep them company. But there can never be any real interchange or mutual sharing. These characters cannot listen compassionately to our grievances and give benevolent advice or encouragement. They only feed parasitically on our time and emotions. We may think we are being entertained or even enlightened but in most cases we are being distracted from a better option – actively participating in life. No wonder the mind-numbing effects of television often serve to re-inforce depression. **We are living in a voyeuristic**

age where people want to be 'peeping Toms' in other peoples' lives without the messiness or heartache of involvement or commitment. We have become afraid of one another – afraid of rejection, provocation and stealing other peoples' precious time if not sacrificing our own, and so we tend to keep ourselves to ourselves. We are afraid of the messiness of commitment and true involvement in other peoples' lives. We watch films where terrible rows or scenes of aggression are enacted while we sit passively or with morbid interest, yet unable to intervene. This causes a vicious cycle of having our emotions stirred, yet doing nothing about them. But emotions were meant to be spurs to action. No wonder so many end up like the living dead, numb and ineffectual like zombies, only imagining what it would be like to do things but never actually doing them.

Life is a lot like watching TV. You have the remote control which is the power to participate and concentrate or not. Some people have the TV on as background but are not focusing which leads to wasted energy and lack of fulfilment. Others keep hopping from one channel to the next, not really sure which path to pursue. Others keep the same channel on religiously even when they are not gaining anything from it – they're in a rut! Some are content to watch fuzzy pictures, and never get the TV fixed so they go through life confused and with lack of clarity. **To a large extent how much TV we watch**

is a barometer of how much we are willing to be a spectator on life or an active participant. But what remains undeniable is that we can never recover the time we have lost.

True Beauty

God has given us all different physiques, but society sends out pervasive messages , largely through media promotion and advertising , that there is a right way , and therefore by implication , a wrong way to look. But the Bible indicates that God purposely created each individual to certain specifications - "Your hands fashioned and made me ...You clothed me with skin and flesh , and knit me together with bones and sinews."[87] All manner of exercising , calorie-counting , vitamin-pill popping, primping and preening should serve to achieve the desirable goal of making us feel at home in the body that God has given us. But **looks can never take precedence over our state of health (spiritual, physical or emotional) for this is what ultimately determines our quality of life.**

We live in a world where we are told image is everything. The unfortunate implication is that its opposite – substance – means nothing. We must be weary - so the lesson goes – of the indirect meaning as well as the direct meaning of our statements and popular jargon. **If substance means nothing, then what's happening inside our bodies and minds is of no consequence as long as we look**

good on the outside. The modelling industry is an obvious example of this skewed way of looking at life. The industry has demanded and sanctioned ultra-thin bodies with skeletal frames while ignoring the ramifications for the models' long-term health. Then there are those who not just look anorexic but are genuinely anorexic out of a desperate quest to be thin at all costs. There is a saying that originated among high society socialites – "you can never be too rich or too thin". This message, though tongue and cheek, can be taken seriously by vulnerable women desperate to stand out from the crowd and be recognised, but for unhealthy reasons.

The shockwaves in the media caused by Kate Moss's statement "nothing tastes as good as skinny feels" was more surprising from its impact than the actual admission.[88] Surely such an extreme view is to be expected from a woman who has earned fame and fortune from her image in an industry where getting fat is akin to a crime. Seemingly, the modelling industry's standards have infiltrated mainstream society to such an extent that many young girls will view 'looking like Kate Moss' as a worthy and feasible goal. But for a relative minority, it will become an obsession. As I surfed a pro-anorexia website as part of my research, I alighted on one of the testimonials of the members. Her reason for regurgitating the chocolate bar that her father had given her, once he had left the room, was that she wanted to stand out when she was walking down the street. At the root of her *body dysmorphia* (an obvious symptom of anorexia whereby she has a distorted perception of her body size and shape) and cunning behaviour to support her extreme dieting, was the longing personal validation and a sense of significance. Pictures of thin celebrities emblazon these websites. Their fans feed off the fact that these women are in the limelight and attract the spotlight; they long for the validation that society is giving them, and conclude that they too must look like them, in order to gain similar validation. The irony is that some of these very cultural icons have found self-esteem and self-acceptance to be just as elusive. Some such as Jane Fonda and Marie Osbourne have publicly admitted to their past eating disorders. Others such as Karen Carpenter, whose deliciously sultry voice, has delighted us for decades with such hits as *There's a kind of hush* and *Close to you*, did not live to triumph against the stronghold of bulimia. So many think they will find validation by standing out from the crowd, whether through the way they look, their academic or financial successes or even the extent of their humanitarian work and charitable giving

A look at any typical music video will reveal that the women are by far more sparsely dressed than the men. There is an inherent contradiction in the way female singers and dancers 'strut their stuff' in a sexy fashion to lyrics which spout empowerment and independence. The style of dressing and seductive posing conveys the message loud and clear that they want to be noticed by men and they do care what men think. This pours cold water on the notion of independence.

The word 'image' denotes more than just external appearance. After all, nature is replete with images – trees, flowers, animals – all have external features which help to identify them. Yet, they are by no means image-conscious. **We humans are the only species that seek to feign an image that does not reflect the truth of who we are.** The word 'image' for us has come to connote falseness and deceit. When we assume an image, we are really playing with peoples' minds and trying to manipulate the way they view us. Implicit in this behaviour is an insecurity – the fear that we will not be accepted or acceptable as we are.

Isn't it interesting that man was made "in the image of God" and yet we don't know what God looks like? He embodies qualities which cannot be pigeon-holed to particular features or dimensions. When something is truly beautiful, it has an intangible quality. You can't quite put your finger on it. All you know is that you want to be around it. You are magnetically drawn to it. In the final analysis, beauty is to be enjoyed for its effect rather than analysed for its components.

The Internet – A Secret Life

The internet encourages us to see living human beings – their voice, smell, touch, even sharing the same space with them – as an inconvenience. We also lessen our opportunities for social contact. Is it not more worthwhile to attend and participate in a live event such as shopping than purchase goods clinically over the net?

The sad reality is that most parents don't know what their children are watching or reading behind closed doors on the internet. Chat roulette is the latest internet trend to captivate the imaginations of the young, the lonely and the bored. It involves a network of users over the age of sixteen who are able to communicate with one another through chat rooms with webcams. At the click of a button, they can terminate one user and move on to another like the throw of a dice. This may sound harmless, enough but already it is being exploited by sexual predators and desperados to flaunt their bodies and demand visual favours from others[89].

Although the internet was designed to foster and facilitate communication, we must not allow it to become a substitute for face-to-face human interaction.

Chapter 6

The Me-Me Syndrome

Me, myself and I

There's an idol called 'self' which will mark the close of time on earth - "There will be terrible times in the last days. People will be lovers of themselves..."[90]Self-love used to be looked upon as a vice - the equivalent of self-indulgence or selfishness. Nowadays it's considered the crux of self-esteem and mental health. In fact, Jesus' admonition to 'love your neighbour as yourself' takes for granted each person's innate desire for self-preservation.

Ultimately, to love oneself is to realise that, as valid as one's opinions and desires may be, one is a mere part of a greater whole and it may sometimes be in the common interest to put aside one's self-interest. Fundamental though the relationship with oneself may be, it is not the be-all or end-all of a satisfying life. At some point we must relate to others. **Indeed we see ourselves mostly through the mirrors of other people's responses to us.** When what we see reflected back at us is undesirable or frightening , we tend to blame the person who is acting as the mirror instead of addressing the cause of the reflection - ourselves. This often explains why we take an unreasonable dislike to someone. Proverbial wisdom captures this idea -"just as water reflects the face, so one human heart reflects another."[91]

The Lure Of Self-Improvement

I grew up on a staple diet of popular psychology. One of the first self-help books I remember reading was 'How to Win Friends and Influence People' by Dale Carnegie. This book whet my appetite for more of the same as self-improvement became my *raison d'etre*. I have come to realise that people who are drawn to this literary fodder have issues with self-inadequacy. At the time, this inadequacy – not feeling quite good enough – was a deficiency which had to be cured. But over the years of arguable over-consumption of these books, with no durable lessening of these feelings, I realised that too much knowledge cannot change a person from the inside. You can change your life from the outside – learn how to speak right, walk and dress right, even think right, yet you could still be plagued with fundamental issues which cut to the very core of your identity. Only God can change that.

It's not that I hadn't been introduced to the Lord from an early age. At fourteen, I became a born-again believer in spite of the fact that I had been going to church since I was a child. Although I had the assurance of salvation, I knew nothing of what the lifestyle of a disciple of Christ really entailed. About fifteen years later, I was planted in a strong church and have discovered the meaning of spiritual warfare. It is based on the reality that we have a spiritual enemy who is bent on our destruction (spiritual, physical and emotional), and who must be resisted at all costs.

Paradigm Shift

Although Dale Carnegie professed faith in Christ himself and his self-help books focused solidly on the scriptures, so often popular self-help manuals fall short of establishing a moral context for living. In fact, many are void of any mention of the word God, much less Jesus, preferring to use the vague terminology of the "universe", "spirit", "mother earth", "Infinite Light" and the like. Yet the quest for fulfilment becomes somewhat futile without a sense of the eventual purpose of human existence. Are you just going to improve yourself so that you can have the best possible opportunities for a happy, trouble-free existence in the here and now, or do you want the assurance that that you are pleasing God in the process because you know He will judge your life.

Christ devotees like myself who have jumped on the self-improvement bandwagon, were living a lie because we lacked knowledge of God through his word. **Self-inadequacy is a reality of life for every man born with the sinful nature.** Why? Because "all have sinned and fallen short of the glory of God." Without Him we can do nothing of ourselves that is of any eternal value. Yes, you may think you're doing a lot; in fact, your CV may be quite impressive to your fellow-man. Yet, in God's eyes, it's all dross. If you want to live the glorious life God intended you to live, then you must learn to think like God. The only manual necessary for this task is the Word of God.

Thinking like God will mean you incur the rejection of your fellow-men. How many are willing to pay that price? God does not value the things we value. That's why He seems so distant, when in reality, we're so distant from Him. Even God looked down on earth to find a man who pursued righteousness, and He couldn't even find one. In the end he decided to come in the likeness of His son to show us how to be righteous and through his death in our place (the consequence of sin is death or eternal separation from God), reconcile us back to the Father. We don't like to hear these truths because they make us feel even more inadequate. Jesus suffered at the hands of men to the point of crucifixion even though he wasn't guilty of any offence, much less any deserving death. His only offence was showing people the folly of their ways. **When we listen to a motivational speaker or read a self-help book, we tend to feel instantly better, but when we're convicted of truth it leaves a bitter after-taste.** The question then arises, what are we going to do with the truth we've heard? The answer is that there's nothing we can do, because it has all been done for us. Acknowledging this fact means letting go of our pride which we hold so dearly. We cannot impress God with our good works and kind postures because He sees into the deep recesses of the heart. The only thing is to believe – that is all he asks of us, to believe in the finished work of the cross to reconcile man to God through the sacrifice of His perfect Son. Consequently those who make a profession of faith in Jesus Christ will be regarded by God as His sons and daughters. This is the joy of divine adoption.

'What do you want to do with your life?' is the much publicised question of New Age spirituality. It is not – 'what would God have me do with my life?' It is possible to achieve many individual goals, live a life of adventure, worldly influence and prestige, all of which may bring you personal satisfaction and pride as well as admiration and approval from others. Yet, you would still have missed the mark if you failed to achieve the ultimate purpose – the purpose for which God made you. You can steamroll into the future on a wing and a prayer, doing whatever suits you best. **Seeking for divine wisdom means having to admit our own human limitation, and to acknowledge that we need assistance outside ourselves to thrive**.

Just as there are natural seasons, we experience fluctuations in our state of mind. For example, it is natural to feel sad when you lose a friend, or to feel angry when you have been betrayed. If you're too positive, you won't allow negative emotions to surface, and therefore be dealt with, for example emotions such as depression, blame and self-pity.

These emotions, if they are persistent, usually point to areas of our lives which need attention.

Popular psychology encourages us to create realities of our own choosing. By so doing, we may reject or distort ultimate reality. Jesus demonstrated reality in a light which conflicts with our natural human instincts. Indeed, the gospel message was bound to raise a few eyebrows because it shook the very foundations of human logic. For example, though Jesus was acclaimed as the 'Prince of Peace', becoming his follower may cause waves in one's family. He challenged the time-worn institution of family life – "I have not come to bring peace but a sword..."[92]. Similarly, He turned our preconceptions of greatness on their heels by equating it with service – "whosoever wants to be first must be last of all and servant of all"[93]. He also admonished his followers to pray for their enemies, and to feed them rather than exact vengeance.

The Need For Balance

In our busy modern lives, we have no time to eat together, share intimate moments with our spouses, to foster friendships or to get to know our neighbours. Narcissism used to be considered a personality disorder, but now it has become typical of those in western, capitalist democracies. The narcissist is in a constant quest for "personal adequacy, power and prestige"[94] It refers to anyone consumed with "vanity, conceit, egotism or simple selfishness."[95]

The Bible never advocates hating yourself, but rather extending yourself. Indeed, you cannot give away what you do not possess. Hence, you can never really give a sense of self-worth to someone else if you lack it yourself. This is particularly essential for parents and leaders. When Jesus came to 'save' us it was to make us 'whole' and 'sound' which is what the original Greek word 'sozo' means. Ultimately all self-pre-occupation must be tempered by the awareness that although each person's views matter, no-one is the centre of the universe but rather part of a greater whole. To forget oneself from time to time, and focus on the greater whole, will logically benefit the whole including oneself. After all, humility is not thinking less of yourself, but thinking of yourself less. But it also involves becoming aware of one's own limitations.

Invariably, it takes set-backs such as ill-health, an emotional or financial crisis for us to regain the proper perspective of God's infinite power compared to our limited abilities. It is indisputable that we cannot control the past, the future or our fellow-men. In His omnipotence, omnipresence and omniscience, God can see the bigger picture of our lives. So to lead abundant lives, it stands to reason that we need to tap into this awesome power - "Whoever would approach God must believe that He exists and that He rewards those who seek Him."[96] No pilot of sound mind would dare fly a plane without links to the control tower, yet so many of us embark on a life without close communication with our Creator. The 'take-control-of -your-life' credo of capitalist, western thinking tends to give us an exaggerated sense of our own capabilities. On life's journey, we all need a compass to keep us headed in the right direction.

All God requires of us is faith in Him. Yet many protest that even this is too much. The reality is that none of us can survive without faith to some degree. From the time we come into this world, we implicitly trust that our needs will be met – that we will be fed, cleaned and clothed. As we get older we have faith that we will get sufficient training to find a job. Without this conviction, we would lack the motivation to apply for training courses or job vacancies, let alone leave the security of the parental home.

Faith is also manifest in other, more subtle ways. We pick up our prescriptions from the chemist and pop them unquestioningly into our mouths without the foggiest notion of what's in them. We allow medical practitioners to invade and tamper with our bodies during minor and major surgical procedures simply because we assume they are qualified. How many of us double-check these qualifications. We hop aboard trains and airplanes not knowing whether the driver has had too much to drink or is suffering the side-effects of medication.

It is clear that we don't have a problem showing

faith. The question is in what or whom do we place our faith. You can only believe in God wholeheartedly if you have proven Him to be 100% reliable. People can only be judged to be unreliable if they have broken a promise made, not what you wanted them to do or would have liked them to have offered to do. If someone you know promises you a gift yet to be delivered, the only reason for having faith in the promise, is the dependability of the promiser - in other words, the degree to which they have promised before and delivered.

Human Rights Gone Crazy

The 1948 universal Declaration of Human Rights sets out the most fundamental of human freedoms such as freedom of speech, freedom of conscience, the right to privacy, freedom of association and the right to life. For these basic human rights, there's a countervailing responsibility for those who claim to be disciples of Christ. For example, they're no longer free to say whatever they like. Rather, their speech must be "flavoured with salt" and edifying. Freedom of thought is replaced by the injunction to think about "whatsoever things are true, whatsoever things are noble, of good report".[97] They are expected to take every thought captive to obey Christ. "[98]

Disciples of Christ are freed from the bondage of sin. They have given all the burdens of their souls to Christ -"If the Lord Jesus shall make you free, you shall be free indeed". God not only separates them from their sins, the source of shame and condemnation("as far as the east is from the west") but through the gift of the Holy Spirit, He empowers us to choose good when faced with the choice between good and evil. The Apostle Paul warned "do not use your freedom as an excuse to indulge in sin". This is how the freedom of the world contrasts with Christian freedom. The world sees freedom as a doorway to self-expression and self-indulgence. By contrast, God sees freedom as a doorway to self-denial. Followers of Christ learn to see sin the way God sees it – a life-threatening disease with the capacity to cause untold human suffering and misery and ultimately separate one eternally from God.

This may lead to the question of whether the fundamental human rights enshrined in all authentic democracies do not apply to disciples of Christ? Indeed, followers of Christ are still expected to obey all earthly authorities as God has allowed them to come to power. The only exception would be where these authorities deliberately flout God's laws as in the case of Daniel in Babylon under King Nebucchadnezzar. Jesus' sermon on the Mount established higher laws which encourage his disciples to go the second mile. Human laws are essentially in place to avoid anarchy. Essentially, they avoid minimum evil and pursue minimum good. God's laws avoid maximum evil and pursue maximum good.

All The Time In The World

Deadlines are often viewed as undesirable time constraints. But they are really externally- imposed reality checks. They serve the purpose of giving meaning and structure to our lives. Think how anarchic society would become if we had all the time in the world to do whatever we want. Some would become permanent couch potatoes or would never work but be on a never-ending cruise - cruising through life like there's no tomorrow. But life is too short and there is too much at stake to justify such a lifestyle.

In community life, there will always be obligations. Any relationship will prompt a set of obligations or duties. The most pervasive ideology of the times in which we live, is that the 'self' is at the centre of the universe. Life therefore becomes self-centred where everything individuals think, say and do must service their needs first and foremost. The danger of this is that we only really see and acknowledge others when there is a crisis in our own lives.

There is a prevailing notion that peace comes with self-acceptance. This overlooks the truth that there will always be aspects of ourselves we need to work to change rather than complacently accept. **We can be lulled into a false sense of peace and security if we believe people should take us or leave us as we are.** This 'like it or lump it' attitude creates a society where we cast off our obligations to others and so many human needs go unmet. This was never God's plan.

'Pick And Mix' Ethics

We have dethroned God and set up our own kingdom where Christ occupies the same position as other sages and saints like Mother Theresa, Ghandi or Buddha. **We pick and choose the bits of wisdom which we like and form a patchwork quilt of beliefs to feed our egos, and make us feel better about ourselves.** Because the 'self' is both the creator and the created, it becomes logical that the individual can both seek and gain forgiveness from himself. The concept of forgiving oneself has become all the rage. You often hear the words "you need to forgive yourself" yet little emphasis is put on seeking forgiveness from the victims of your crimes and misdemeanours, or from God who imparts a conscience to all men – His laws are written on our hearts. Some proponents of New Age spirituality have even gone so far as to say we can forgive ourselves for ever thinking we did anything wrong.

In the name of positive thinking traditional vices have been morphed into virtues. For example, jealousy is perceived as a helpful clue to areas of your life where you are harbouring unfulfilled ambitions. We are being encouraged to indulge emotions which left unchecked could lead to the destruction of relationships, and crimes of passion resulting in death. 'Justification' or the process of being made right with God is less of a priority than feeling good about yourself. Many disciples of Christ experience the cross as a way of feeling good about themselves by being valued by a God who loves them so much that He sent his son to die for them. They do not see it primarily as a place of repentance where there is genuine contrition over their sins. Yet, it is a deep conviction of one's sinfulness and how much it offends God that leads to genuine repentance. We will be content to remain as we are if we only view ourselves as weak and prone to errors which are covered up by a kind and understanding Saviour.

Exit On Demand

The danger of thinking that your life is yours to do with as you please, and that ultimately the only one you can rely on is 'me, myself and I', is that, taken to its full extent, you will tend to regard suicide as a viable option when life no longer makes sense. Suicide (death at one's own hands) can be slow or sudden and is the ultimate expression of self-hatred. It may take the form of slow starvation, a destructive compulsion or be the result of a sudden impulse to do away with yourself. Our relationship with ourselves, in terms of what we think and say about ourselves, is fundamental to our well-being. After all, it is what we tell ourselves that will permeate our sub-conscious minds and determine our behaviour. No human being can know you the way you know yourself, and only you can decide whether you will share that knowledge with another.

To know yourself is to understand your motivations which arise from your desires as well as your behaviour which arises from your fears. We tend to opt for the deceptively safe haven of 'denial' because dealing with the unsavoury aspects of ourselves can be painful. For a silent majority, suicide is a taboo subject to be treated with a mixture of contempt and denial. Although suicidal thoughts may enter our minds at some time or another, fortunately only a relative few actually follow through with the plan or impulse. Nevertheless, even one suicide is an irreplaceable loss of human potential. **The high incidence of suicide across the globe is an indictment on the prevailing attitude that life is for the survival of the fittest, thereby marginalizing those who are physically or mentally weak or disabled.** But the Bible encourages us to support the weak -"We who are strong ought to put up with the failings of the weak..."[99]

Chapter 7

The Pursuit of a Pure Life Strategy

You may think it's impossible to live a pure life. For a long time I would tend to have agreed with you because I stumbled along the way. The good news is that when you make a mistake, you can go to God and confess. He wipes the slate clean, so you can start anew. When you discover the truths - "Blessed are the pure in heart for they will see the Lord"[100] and "Live a clean life, if you don't, you will never see the Lord"[101], what more incentive do you need? When our spiritual eyes are enlightened, we will truly see God for who He is, see ourselves for who we are and appreciate how much we need God. It is when our spiritual sight is restored that we can truly shout 'I was blind but now I see'. The culture of the day is pre-occupied with external sight-seeing in the form of the blockbuster film, the hottest celebrity, exotic holiday destinations, the latest model of car and this season's fashion must-haves. Those who have seen enough of what this culture has to offer know that these sights do not offer lasting satisfaction. I wouldn't want to miss out on the ultimate feel-good spectacle – the Creator of the universe Himself. Purity is what will qualify us for this. Let this be your motivation, as it is mine.

To clear our minds of all the clutter, baggage

and deceptions we've been accumulating over the course of our lives, we must undergo a spiritual detox programme. We have to determine to exclude or diminish certain activities from our lives such as technological stimulation, and incorporate more of the wholesome stuff such as prayer, journaling, reading, meditation, nature exploration. We can learn to befriend silence - an indispensable tool in the attainment of purity. You will discover sounds you never noticed before and learn to attune to God's voice. You will learn to hear the voice of your conscience instead of drowning it out with activity. Closing your eyes to the images of the world, which so often assault the soul, will open up a panorama of spiritual insight and foresight. God will give you deep revelation about the present and the future. The person in pursuit of the pure life is more interested in seeing inwardly than outwardly.

Let's face it, purity doesn't just happen overnight anymore than weight-loss, unless you're a prisoner of war in Cambodia or suffering from an undesirable illness. We have to take steps to avoid impure thoughts, sights, sounds. We have to do some forward planning, and anticipate certain obstacles. Listening to the sounds of nature as opposed to the synthesised sounds created by our various technological gadgets, helps us to stay in tune with God, ourselves and our fellow man. John Naish in his article 'Is anyone out there listening? ' observes that "An increasingly common response is for us to "bubble" ourselves inside a pair of headphones, so that at least the noise we hear is self-selected. But this urge for aural control takes us away from the habit of listening for the ambient and the unexpected."[102]

Reality Check

All my life I've been tempted by women's magazines and celebrity glossies. They helped me escape from the humdrum and the downright depressing into a more glamorous, exciting reality. Or so I thought. I've already shared (chapter 5: Media Mayhem) how bit by bit I began to see this world for what it was – shallow and empty. It promised much but delivered little. Celebrity couples I had idolised became divorced, or the celebrities were seen in less flattering lights – without make-up or doing something stupid. They were human after all. I had been wrong to idolize them as they were not worthy of my unquestioning adoration.

Every now and then we must take a reality check. The last day of each month is a good time, but you can also do it daily by bedtime purging - confession and repentance. Share with the Lord what you struggled with today, what tempted you. For many years I was caught up in a virtual reality. Jumping on the celebrity bandwagon, and wanting to keep up-to-date with my favourite celebs was not reality. I had never met these people and so didn't know what they were really like. Rather I was relying on third party information.

Much of the information was to promote something they were trying to sell. They hired publicists in the hope that I wouldn't find out something they would rather I didn't know or would cast the celebrities in a disparaging light as if to convey that they were only human after all. In recent years, it seems that the more dirt is dug up about a celebrity the more appealing they become. The human side of us – the side that doesn't look so good in the morning, that makes stupid mistakes or gets fat and wrinkly is the reality we must accept and embrace. At the very least, it keep us humble. I read articles written weeks or months prior to release attached to photos taken weeks or even years before. So much may have changed in that person's life since then.

I needed to reclaim reality by focusing on the moment. This meant returning to the present demands and challenges of my life. The aim must be to get the most out of the moment. It is over the immediate moment that I can exercise the most power. My future which sometimes fills me with anxiety and dread, consists of the moments of my life. The person in search of the pure life, always looks at the bigger picture. Long-term rewards are preferred over short-term pleasures. Giving into temptation can only ever yield a temporary buzz, but then comes regret and consequences.

The stronghold of my life has been the temptation to engage in escapism whether through television, film, magazines or fantasy. What is the bee/scorpion which bites you every time? It might be the lure of casual sex or pornography, or falling for the deception that more money or education will make you happier. Whatever your Achilles heel, it sets you up for a rude awakening when reality eventually bites and all your illusions come crashing down.

With so many worldly distractions and temptations you must have substitutes and a plan B. What did Joseph do when Potiphar's wife made her indecent proposal? He fled at the expense of the shirt on his back.[103] Apostle Paul seconds this with his appeal to flee youthful lusts. Back to the 'fight-or-flight' reaction. It's interesting that Paul didn't say fight it, but rather flee. Get away from what's tempting you. Close the magazine, click the mouse or press the off switch. Don't just sit passively and toy with it in your mind.

Here are some everyday scenarios to consider. How do you typically deal with them? What are the alternatives?

Scenario 1: No point getting home at the end of a tough day, dog-tired, flop in front of the television and begin to channel hop. That is a recipe for falling into temptation. If you happen to engage in mindless channel-hopping after the 9pm watershed, you may be in for an even greater shock.

Alternative: nature – God's treasure chest of natural comforts – the fresh air, the gentle breeze, the warm sunshine, the refreshing rain, the relaxing stretch of green.

Scenario 2: Feeling restless. Don't leg it to blockbusters or hot foot it to the fridge for some comfort food or to the mall for some retail therapy.

Alternative: Put on your walking shoes or sit in the garden. Resist the temptation to take your mobile or your ipod. Focus on the sounds of nature. Quietness and reflection are essential precursors to purity. They help to fine-tune our sense of discernment when we are bombarded with too much sensory stimulation.

Scenario 3: You walk into a takeaway shop and see posters of bikini-clad women all over the walls. This happened to me. It used to bug me because I couldn't keep my eyes away from these provocative images. I complained to one of the assistants, but it seemed to fall on deaf ears. One day many years later, the shop had been revamped by new management. Hallelujah, the posters had gone.

Alternative: If the fire is too hot, turn off the stove or get out of the kitchen. There are some places where you cannot as a Christian comfortably be. Paul said that we mustn't use our liberty as an opportunity for the flesh.[104] By law, you may have every right to be there but is it worth it if it's going to tempt you to sin? My husband and I decided we would stop going to the cinema. We love films, but have had to curtail our viewing significantly as we have become more sensitive to sin. We also found that the previews were the most challenging aspect of going to the pictures as we were bombarded by images from other films we would never dream of watching. This may not offend every Christ seeker, but we must be sensitive to the Holy Spirit's leading and our own weaknesses.

Scenario 4: you buy a film or CD which you thought was wholesome, but turns out not to be. Do you keep it, sell it, give it away or throw it away?

Alternative: It's hard to throw something away when we've invested money in it. But passing it on to someone else would be knowingly giving them something you think is harmful or less than edifying. The truth is that living the pure life will cost you something. Some lessons are more expensive than others. Throwing it away will make you less prone to buying something without proper inspection in the future. When you look at it that way, you're actually saving money.

Profile Of A Celebrity Junkie (Questionnaire)

- Do you turn to the gossip column of the paper first?
- Can you not go to the supermarket without gravitating to the magazine rack?

- Do you look forward to going to the dentist so that you can read the free magazines in the waiting room?
- Do you have to do a Google search on a celebrity from time to time when you've seen them on a billboard or heard their name mentioned in television or in a conversation?
- Do you always have an opinion when conversation turns towards a celebrity?
- Do your ears prick up when you hear the celebrity mentioned in other peoples' conversations or on the news or radio?
- Do you veer towards the celebrity biographies in the bookstore or department?

A Day Without Technology

I wanted to see how I would get by without listening to my ipod on walks and in the car or while doing housework; no internet connection; no mobile phone; no listening to CDs in the car. I fell off the bandwagon so many times until it finally dawned on me that I needed to plan ahead:

Pursuit Of A Pure Life Strategy

- Start the day with a tune in your head - something wholesome. Keep singing that tune such as a hymn throughout the day.

- Carry a journal to jot down thoughts at a moment's notice. This helps you to arrange your thoughts logically. Disorganised, random thoughts engender anxiety.
- You may still need to carry your mobile for emergencies. At least try to have moments in the day when your phone is switched off such as during meals and prayer time.
- See how you can substitute phone calls with old-fashioned, handwritten letters, cards, postcards or just praying for someone or a situation. What is it that you really want to say to your friend?
- The thought of not being privy to the daily news might fill you with panic, so ask a friend/spouse to let you know if anything major or life-changing happens.
- Interrupt your thoughts with words, for example, "excuse me, Carla, what do you mean by that?"
- Realistically you may need to eliminate one piece of technology rather than all. For example start with something feasible such as no CDs or radio in the car. Learn to savour the silence or talk to others, pray out loud.

Coming Off A Techno Fast

- Carry a selection of wholesome CDs in the car.
- Try instrumental music without lyrics
- Your ipod can be a useful device for counteracting background noise such as music in the shops which isn't wholesome.

Confession 1

When I was reading some news on the internet, I went on the Daily Mail website saved to my 'Favourites'. Instantly I was assaulted with exposed bodies – the latest celebrity body critique which encouraged me towards image consciousness. I had learned too well that images lie because they can tell you whatever you want to see. I made the bold step of not just clicking the exit button but deleting that news site from my favourites.

Lesson: Know your areas of weaknesses, and avoid situations which exploit them.

Deception: the pursuit of the perfect body will fulfil us.

Confession 2

I fantasised about what it would be like to be a certain celebrity and to be in her shoes - her looks, her career, her clothes, her husband/boyfriend.

Lesson: envying others makes us disregard the negatives about them and the positives about ourselves.

Deception: the grass is greener on the other side. The life of a celebrity is better than yours by virtue of their celebrity.

Reality is where the truly great God moments can occur

Bedtime Routine

We all have rituals which we observe before we go to bed, some more detailed than others. This is a critical time of the day because the thoughts we fall asleep with will influence our dreams and the mood with which we awake the following day. It's very tempting to:

- Fall into bed and switch off the lights
- Channel hop
- Fall prey to the munchies
- Sip Ovaltine, hot chocolate or other calming, non-alcoholic beverage.

What we feel obliged to do:

- Brush our teeth.

- Wash our face.
- Take a shower.
- Choose wardrobe for next day.
- Put on face and hand cream.

An equivalent spiritual routine (just before falling asleep when all physical activity is complete):

- Have a *tête*-à-*tête* with your Creator.
- You can be as real as you want to be because he already knows all about you, but He wants you to feel close enough to open up willingly.
- Wipe the slate of the day clean by seeking forgiveness. According to the Lord's prayer, we extend forgiveness to others then ask for God's forgiveness for ourselves.
- Pray for strength for tomorrow. The spectre of tomorrow can make cowards of us all, that is why Jesus advised his followers to take one day at a time. If you are struggling to fall asleep, it may be you are worrying about tomorrow's challenges. Write down your top three fears, then prayerfully release them to god in prayer. Close your eyes and envisage them floating away on a cloud, higher and higher until you can no longer see them.
- Journal thoughts and experiences of the day

and dreams for tomorrow.

- Pray for strength for tomorrow.
- Having water by the bed is comparable to having a purifying scripture to meditate on because God's word cleanses our spirits.
- It's a good idea to turn off all electrical outlets from the wall before bed(such as TV, phone, lamp, computer) because of the electro-magnetic radiation which can disturb sleep.

Fruit Fast

A fruit fast helps to cleanse the inner mind. The fruit of the spirit are:

- Love
- Joy
- Peace
- Patience
- Goodness
- kindness
- Gentleness
- Faithfulness
- Self-control.[105]

Choose a day where you focus on one particular fruit and ask the Holy Spirit to develop this particular fruit in your life so you will have a Christ-like spirit.

A regular fitness programme is an essential part of any effective physical detoxification plan. Perhaps up until this point your exercise has consisted of:

- Chewing junk food.
- Walking to the fridge and back
- Typing on the computer.
- Texting on your mobile phone.
- Talking to friends on the phone.

None of the above will improve your heart rate and cause you to sweat out impurities. Here are some of the spiritual habits and activities we must avoid:

- Competitiveness.
- Fluctuating emotions.
- False dramas/histrionics.
- Gossip/gibberish.
- Extravagance.
- Chaos.
- Judgement

Instead we must seek to replace them with the following:

- Service to others and a team spirit.
- Serenity.

- Humility.
- Listening/brevity.
- Thriftiness.
- Order.
- Acceptance.

Daily Prayer

You might want to use the following prayer as a template for your own daily conversations with God.

Heavenly Father,

You are the embodiment of purity. Show me how to live a pure life that is acceptable to You. Help me to let go of the toxic influences of this world. Help me to develop the mind of Christ so I can think your thoughts and so my life will not be fashioned on just good ideas but God ideas. Lead me in the centre of your perfect will for my life all my days, today and always. I pray this through your son, Jesus Christ, who demonstrated the beauty of pure living.

Amen

Epilogue

This earthly life is the training ground for purity. Of the new earth or new Jerusalem, Jesus says "nothing defiled shall enter its gates." It's now or never, but this should not fill us with dread. Who would want to go to university forever? There will come a time when we will either graduate or be kicked out. The prospect of death gives us a time limit on getting it right. God knows our intentions. We may make the same mistake over and over, but He knows the deepest longings of our soul and whether or not we really want to be pure. There is no better illustration of this fact than King David. God described him as a man after God's own heart, yet David committed some big 'whoppers'. He lusted after a married woman, had an adulterous affair with her, then killed her husband to cover up her pregnancy.

Just as it is impossible for a human-being to stop growing or ageing physically, spiritual growth is necessary if life is to be rewarding. There is no question of going backwards, and although we may feel we are going around in circles, this is simply because we are being given many opportunities to learn familiar but difficult lessons. Indeed, the experiences of life do not guarantee maturity, but rather it is the conclusions that we draw from those experiences that inform our growth. We tend to stay within our comfort zones because growth is usually accompanied by a degree of discomfort. To step outside a comfort zone spells a voyage into the unknown with attendant risks, and as is the case with an athlete in training, pain is a great disincentive to forward motion. Leaving the familiarity of our comfort zones is like emerging from a dark cave into the blinding light. Inhabiting the light is much more enjoyable than the darkness , but there is an initial period of adjustment during which it is all too tempting to cower back into familiar though unsatisfying territory . The scripture offers this reminder to Christ devotees - "For once you were darkness, but now in the Lord you are light . Live as children of light - for the fruit of the light is found in all that is good and right and true."[106]

Those who experience the satisfaction of fulfilling their potential resist such temptation on a regular basis. Our lives will take shape naturally according to our faith and our vision. Our lives are limited, not so much by our circumstances, as by our poverty of imagination and vision. Many of us think that in order to evaluate our progress we should look around us and see how we are doing in relation to our peers, but we are better served by looking to see from whence we have come then how much further we have to go to reach our goals. The Apostle Paul demonstrated this attitude in his statement - "...this one thing I do: forgetting what lies behind and straining forward to what lies ahead."[107]

We cannot allow a celebrity of the moment to

set our moral compass, bearing in mind that in 50 years' time, they will not wield the influence they currently have. Another celebrity will take their place in our affections, and the celebrity bandwagon, though exciting at first, will eventually give way to disillusionment.

Whatever you are exposed to in the world whether a form of art or man-made technology, here's a litmus test of whether or not it promotes purity:

- Does it inspire me to go out and be an activist or lapse into the observer, day-dreamer role of a pacifist?
- What would Jesus do? Instead, would I be willing to share in this activity with Jesus? Jesus rubbed shoulders with the wretched, downcast and worst of sinners but he did not indulge in their sins.
- Does it restore my soul or deplete it?

The benefits of purity are immeasurable. Instead of wasting time being captive to sin, and having to be pulled out of the mire by a gracious, forgiving Father, we can use our earth time constructively to focus on why we're really here. Sin is for so many a pleasurable, promising detour or short-cut which ends up derailing their destinies. Many have dabbled in sex, drugs and alcohol, body fanaticism, hero worship and the like only to end up prematurely dead or permanently disillusioned. Lives have been needlessly shipwrecked for a temporary feel-good factor.

So many have 'become Christians' without realising they also signed up for purity. Becoming a disciple of Christ requires a disciplined mind. You have to deny yourself the things you are naturally inclined to do. There has to come a point when you realise that all the world has to offer is not what it's cracked up to be. We are told "do not love the world or the things in the world...the lust of the flesh, the lust of the eyes, and the pride of life."[108] The good news is that Jesus promises to wash us clean when we give him our hearts – the place where wrong desires and appetites begin. Think about it **– if he could break the chains of death, there is no habit which holds you captive from which he cannot deliver you.** Submission to him has the power to transform our whole identities – we become new creatures in Christ. I hope you will continue to pray for me on my journey of purity as I pray for you. Remember, with God all things are possible.

Notes

1 Wikipedia, "Culture," http://en.wikipedia.org/wiki/Culture (accessed May 26, 2010).

2 Philippians 2:15.

3 Arthur Murphy, The Works of Cornelius Tacitus, with an essay on his life and genius, notes, supplements etc. (Philadelphia, Thomas Wardle: 1836), 287.

4 James 2:2-4.

5 Matthew 6:24.

6 Matthew 4:8.

7 James 1:17.

8 Proverbs 10:22.

9 1 John 2:15-16(NLT).

10 1 Timothy 6:8.

11 Ecclesiastes 7:8.

12 The Oprah Winfrey Show, "Whitney Houston Tells All," http://www.oprah.com/entertainment/Oprah-Exclusive-Interview-with-Whitney-Houston (accessed September 10, 2010).

13 Kristi Watts, "Natalie Cole: Faith in Her Heavenly Father," http://www.cbn.com/cbnmusic/interviews/700club_nataliecole.aspx (accessed September 10, 2010).

14 Mark 14:7.

15 Hampton Stevens, "Is The Tiger Woods Scandal a sports Story?" http://www.theatlantic.com/culture/archive/2010/03/-the-tiger-woods-scandal-a-sports-story/37900/ (accessed September 13, 2010).

16 Rabbi Shmuley, "Why America is the most depressed Nation earth,", 1 March 1,2010, http://www.shmuley.com/articlesdetails/why_america_is_the_most_depressed_nation_on_earth/ (accessed April 29, 2010).

17 Luke 12:48.

18 Job 1:21(New Century Version).

19 Psalm 46.

20 Committee on Communications, "Children, adolescents, and advertising," http://pediatrics.aappublications.org/cgi/content/full/118/6/2563(accessed December 12, 2006).

21 Hebrews 4: 15-`6.

22 John 1:3.

23 John Bevere, Drawing Near: A Life of Intimacy with God (Thomas Nelson Publishers, 2004), 98.

24 Tim Henley, "President Obama is more popular than Jesus Christ," http://blog.newsok.com/gossip/2009/02/20/president-obama-is-more-popular-than-jesus-christ/,(accessed May 12, 2010).

25 Galatians 4:8.

26 God's intimate relationship with every aspect of His creation is explored in Job 38-39.

27 Madonna, Ray of Light, Maverick, Warner Bros. 0093624684725,1998.

28 IMDb, "Biography for Marilyn Monroe," http://www.imdb.com/name/nm0000054/bio (accessed September 23, 2010).

29 David Ritz, Divided Soul: the Life of Marvin Gaye(London ,united Kingdom: Omnibus Press, , 1995).(Omnibus Press, 1995).

30 To Die For. DVD.Directed by Gus Van Sant.1995;Los Angeles, CA: Columbia Pictures, 1998.

31 Matthew 16:26.

32 1 John 5:21.

33 James 1:23-24.

34 James 2:19.

35 James 2:26.

36 Mark 8:36.

37 Philippians 2:14-15.

38 Ecclesiastes 4:12.

39 BBC News, "Sexualisation 'harms' young girls," http://news.bbc.co.uk/1/hi/health/6376421.stm (accessed April 14, 2007).

40 Linda Papadopoulos, 'Why Do Rihanna's Pop Songs Have to Tell Girls they're 'sluts'?" http://www.dailymail.co.uk/femail/article-1279757/Why-pop-songs-tell-girls-theyre-sluts.html (accessed June 10, 2010).

41 1 John 2: 15-16.

42 Jeannette Kupfermann, "The Sexual Sickness at the heart of our society," The Mail on Sunday (femail), October 13,1996.

43 Genesis 3:17-19.

44 Genesis 3:16.

45 Diana Appleyard, "Househusband backlash as high-flying wives ditch men they wanted to stay at home," http://www.dailymail.co.uk/femail/article-467390/Househusband-backlash-high-flying-wives-ditch-men-em-em-wanted-stay-home.html (accessed July 10, 2007).

46 Fay Weldon, "Why women must fight for the return of He Devils," http://findarticles.com/p/articles/mi_8003/is_1997_May_4/ai_n35800620/ (accessed May 4, 119).

47 Proverbs 14:12.

48 Seana McGee and Marice Taylor: The New Couple: why the old rules don't work and what does.

49 Pepper Schwartz, Peer Marriage: how Love Between Equals really works (The Free Press, US, 1994).

50 1 Corinthians 13: 4-8.

51 Paul Fuller, "Divorce Damages Health," Daily Express, July 18, 1995.

52 Romans 12:3.

53 Romans 3:10.

54 BBC News, "Sexual disease clinics failing," http://news.bbc.co.uk/1/hi/health/4225320.stm (accessed September 8, 2005).

55 Sarah Boseley, "Sexually Transmitted Infections: education is the answer not outrage, The Observer http://www.guardian.co.uk/uk/2010/aug/29/sarah-boseley-sexually-transmitted-diseases (accessed September 10,2010).

56 Angela Lambert, "Just what do these woman tell us about our society, "Daily Mail, August 2, 1997, under "Byline: ANGELA LAMBERT," http://findarticles.com/p/

news-articles/daily-mail-london-england-the/mi_8002/is_1997_August_2/just-women-society/ai_n35822221/?tag=content;col1 (accessed May 26, 2010).

57 SPUC, "Morning-after pill does not lower abortion rates," Pro-life Times, March, 2007.

58 Virginia Ironside, "Can too much intimacy destroy true love?"Daily Mail, Mon November 18, 1996.

59 Robin Norwood, "I was a love junkie but I cured myself,"Daily Mirror, May 12, 1995.

60 Matthew 15:11.

61 Proverbs 10:19.

62 Esther 4:14.

63 1 Samuel 15:1-3.

64 Acts 8:29-35.

65 Proverbs 10:32.

66 Ephesians 6:2.

67 Proverbs 3:16-17.

68 James 1:19.

69 Proverbs 18:7.

70 Proverbs 18:21.

71 Proverbs 16:24.

72 Genesis 9:6.

73 James 3:5-6.

74 CBS News.com, "Music Lyrics Offer Earful About Drugs," http://www.cbsnews.com/stories/2008/02/05/health/webmd/main3790632.shtml (accessed April 2, 2008).

75 James 5:16.

76 2 Timothy 3:16.

77 Dumbing down, "Dumbing Down: Or The Banalisation Of Culture," http://nomuzak.co.uk/dumbing_down.html (accessed May 19, 2010).

78 1 Peter 5:8.

79 Psalm 119: 37.

80 Matthew 5:28.

81 Ephesians 6:11-17.

82 Acts 17:28

83 Matthew 6:10.

84 Mary Ellen Ashcroft, Temptations Women Face: Honest talk about Jealousy, Anger, Sex, Money, Food, Pride (Illinois: Intervarsity press, 1991), 121.

85 Mary Ellen Ashcroft, Temptations Women Face: Honest talk about Jealousy, Anger, Sex, Money, Food, Pride (Illinois: Intervarsity press, 1991), 119.

86 Wikipedia, "Reality Television," http://en.wikipedia.org/wiki/Reality_television (accessed July 13, 2007).

87 Job 10:8-11

88 Alexandra Topping, "Kate Moss's Motto Gives Comfort to 'pro-anorexic' Community," http://www.guardian.co.uk/lifeandstyle/2009/nov/20/kate-moss-motto-pro-aanorexic (accessed May 10, 2010).

89 Olivia Lichtenstein, "when Olivia's daughter told her about a 'cool' new teen website, she decided to investigate. What she found was the most disturbing internet craze yet, "Daily Mail, April 26 2010, pp. 22-23.

90 2 Timothy 3:1-2.

91 Proverbs 27:19

92 Matthew 10: 34-37.

93 Mark 9:35.

94 http://www.google.co.uk/search?q='narcissism'&rls=com.microsoft:*:IE-SearchBox&ie=UTF-8&oe=UTF-8&sourceid=ie7&rlz=1I7SUNA&redir_esc=&ei=_1H9S6OXHpr60wTar_zzBQ (accessed May 26, 2010).

95 Wikipedia, "Narcissism," http://en.wikipedia.org/wiki/Narcissism (accessed 26 May 26, 2010).

96 Hebrews 11:6.

97 Philippians 4: 8.

98 2 Corinthians 10:5.

99 Romans 15:1.

100 Matthew 5:8.

101 Hebrews 12:14 (Contemporary English version).

102 John Naish, "Is anyone out there listening?" http://www.timesonline.co.uk/tol/life_and_style/health/features/article6891004.ece (accessed Nov 5, 2009).

103 Genesis 39:10-1

104 Galatians 5:14.

105 Galatians 5:22-23.

106 Ephesians 5:8-9.

107 Philippians 3:13.

108 1 John 2:15-16.

Also by the Author

Captive Daughters

At a time when so many advocates and activists are lobbying for the enforcement of women's rights and trying to improve their socio-economic status across the globe, it would be all too easy for the emotional and spiritual needs of women to be side-lined. Despite the modern woman's political and educational gains, she still battles certain life-limiting tendencies. Many women are still captive to:

The beauty myth which stems from the misconception that improving their appearance will transform their lives from the outside in, or the belief that their value is determined by how they look.

Choosing inappropriate female role models usually from the glossy industries of entertainment and fashion where style is valued over substance.

Romantic delusions spun by the Hollywood industry where the focus is on 'boy meets girl' then they live happily ever after with no real understanding of what it takes to stay married.

Trying frenetically to juggle the myriad roles they undertake while still finding time to nurture their own souls and maintain physical health and well-being.

These are some of the major challenges women face which represent chains which hold them captive. These chains can only be broken by having the courage to tackle long-held mind-sets and savouring the freedom only to be found in truth-centred thinking

ISBN 978-1-90797-103-7

Time for Me

Every carer, whether family, friend or support worker, needs a daily dose of inspiration to help them face the challenges of caring with fortitude and patience while retaining their sanity. If you fall into this category, this is just the resource for you.

ISBN 978-1-85345-428-8

www.ingramcontent.com/pod-product-compliance
Ingram Content Group UK Ltd.
Pitfield, Milton Keynes, MK11 3LW, UK
UKHW021052270726
13967UKWH00012B/632

9 781907 971006